IRELAND'S HOPE

The "peculiar theories" of James Fintan Lalor

by
James P. Bruce

Series in World History
VERNON PRESS

Copyright © 2021 James P. Bruce.

All rights reserved. No part of this publication may be reproduced, stored in a retrieval system, or transmitted in any form or by any means, electronic, mechanical, photocopying, recording, or otherwise, without the prior permission of the copyright holder and Vernon Art and Science Inc.

www.vernonpress.com

In the Americas:	*In the rest of the world:*
Vernon Press	Vernon Press
1000 N West Street,	C/Sancti Espiritu 17,
Suite 1200, Wilmington,	Malaga, 29006
Delaware 19801	Spain
United States	

Series in World History

Library of Congress Control Number: 2020939819

ISBN: 978-1-64889-171-7

Also available: 978-1-62273-898-4 [Hardback]; 978-1-64889-081-9 [PDF, E-Book]

Product and company names mentioned in this work are the trademarks of their respective owners. While every care has been taken in preparing this work, neither the authors nor Vernon Art and Science Inc. may be held responsible for any loss or damage caused or alleged to be caused directly or indirectly by the information contained in it.

Every effort has been made to trace all copyright holders, but if any have been inadvertently overlooked the publisher will be pleased to include any necessary credits in any subsequent reprint or edition.

Cover design by Vernon Press using elements designed by Nicolas Raymond from freestock.ca (external source from Freepik), aopsan / Freepik.

Image on the back cover: James P. Bruce (left) and Kevin Lalor-Fitzpatrick (right) at the former family home in Co. Laois (formerly Queen's County) where James Fintan Lalor spent most of his life.

Dedicated to Brian Cleeve
(1921-2003)
without whom this would not have been possible

Table of Contents

ABBREVIATIONS   vii

INTRODUCTION   ix

CHAPTER ONE
JAMES FINTAN LALOR'S "PECULIAR VIEWS ON THE TENURE QUESTION"   1
Duties vs. rights: Land tenure in Ireland   1
James Fintan Lalor: Background   5
Academia and Lalor   6
Lalor's early writings   12
Lalor and the Irish Confederation   14
    The *Nation* articles   17
    Lalor's "private exhortations and remonstrances"   22
    Setback at Holy Cross   25
Lalor and *The Irish Felon*   28
    "The Faith of a Felon"   33
Lalor the revolutionary   36
"This island-Queen"   38

CHAPTER TWO
"DESTITUTE OF BOOKS": LALOR'S LITERARY PRECURSORS   43
Inspiration and influence   44
Acquiring "pure English"   46
British radicals and land tenure   48
    William Ogilvie   50
    Thomas Spence   53
    Thomas Paine   56
The United Irishmen   59
Chartism and the Irish   61
    Thomas Ainge Devyr   62

Feargus O'Connor	63
James 'Bronterre' O'Brien	64
Thomas Davis	69
A French connection?	73
1848 and the rise of Socialism	74
Blackstone and Locke	76

CHAPTER THREE
"I SOMETIMES WISH FOR SOME ONE TO SPEAK TO": LALOR AND HIS CONTEMPORARIES

	83
Lalor's peers	83
John Marnell	83
William Conner	85
William Sharman Crawford	89
The Lalors of Tinakill	90
Patrick ('Patt') Lalor: paterfamilias and reformer	91
Richard Lalor: brother and reluctant ally	95
Young Ireland	97
Charles Gavan Duffy	97
Michael Doheny	101
Thomas Devin Reilly	104
John Mitchel	106
Readers of *The Nation* and *The Irish Felon*	120

EPILOGUE	125
CONCLUSION	127
BIBLIOGRAPHY	129
FURTHER READING	141
INDEX	143

Abbreviations

DIB	Dictionary of Irish Biography
IHS	Irish Historical Studies
JFL	James Fintan Lalor
NAI	National Archives of Ireland
NLI	National Library of Ireland
ODNB	Oxford Dictionary of National Biography
PL	Patrick ('Patt') Lalor
RL	Richard Lalor
RIA	Royal Irish Academy
UCD	University College Dublin

INTRODUCTION

Settling on the subject of this book was not straightforward. When I applied to become a DPhil student at Oxford University, I had something different in mind: a kind of intellectual history of nationalism during the period between the death of Charles Stewart Parnell in 1891 and the setting up of the Irish Free State in 1922. I was particularly interested in the economic issues that I felt must have occupied the minds of those contemplating self-government for Ireland. It took me a year to realise that the topic was much too big for a single thesis. However, one minor strand of my preliminary research offered possibilities for a new direction.

I was intrigued by the attention paid by a handful of contemporary writers and activists to the subject of land nationalisation. This was a previously exotic concept brought into mainstream discussion by Henry George's book, *Progress and Poverty*, published in 1879. Among those influenced by George's analysis was Michael Davitt, founder of the Irish Land League. He became an ardent advocate of land nationalisation during the early 1880s. Although the concept never gained much political or popular support in Ireland, before or after independence, it continued to arouse interest amongst a handful of thinkers and observers well into the twentieth century. In my reading I found that, while the impact of Henry George's book was evident in the small body of writings on the subject, the influence of another earlier writer was frequently cited. He was a journalist named James Fintan Lalor. Some commentators saw Lalor as having given land nationalisation a uniquely Irish flavour during the Great Famine of the 1840s. So using Lalor's writings as my starting point, I set out to trace the development of this arcane idea, through the twists and turns of Irish intellectual history, up to its most recent expression in the work of the Kilkenny-born economist, Raymond Crotty.

However, at the halfway stage, my revised research project was derailed by illness. Rather than abandon my work completely, I transferred to the shorter MLitt programme. By then, I had completed a detailed analysis of Lalor's ideas on the twin topics of land tenure and Irish independence. So I submitted the results as my final thesis. The analyses and arguments presented in that thesis form the basis of the present book. What is missing, of course, is a detailed examination of Lalor's influence on later generations of activists, land reformers, and politicians of various hues. Perhaps the brief epilogue at the end of this book will inspire someone else to continue the story.

In the last few years of his life, James Fintan Lalor lived through a momentous period in modern Irish history. In 1845 the arrival of potato blight precipitated the Famine that devastated Ireland for the remainder of the decade. Parts of the country also became embroiled in the revolutionary turmoil that erupted in continental Europe during 1848, although outbreaks of actual violence were rare. During this period Lalor became a leading figure in the Irish Confederation, a group formed by disaffected members of the Loyal National Repeal Association. He is probably best known today as the author of a series of opinion pieces which were published in the major newspapers of the day. These articles have been reprinted and analysed numerous times since then, whether by academics, admirers, or adversaries.

The continuing attention paid to Lalor's writings has not, however, led to any consensus about his political, social, or economic beliefs. There is disagreement on issues such as the extent of his influence on Davitt and the Land League, the degree to which he exhibited socialist leanings, and whether or not he was a proto-land nationaliser. These differences of interpretation extend even to basic biographical details, indicating a level of confusion that seems surprising given how recently Lalor lived and died. The two most significant memorials erected in Lalor's honour illustrate how easily falsehoods about his life are perpetuated.

Inscribed into the headstone placed over his grave in 1948 is an epitaph to:

Séamus Fionntáin Uí Leatlobair
A rugað an 10 ṁað lá de Ṁárta 1809.
Agus a cailleað
an 27 ṁað lá de Ṁí na Nodlag 1849.[1]

The Irish language inscription goes on to eulogise Lalor's patriotism and his sacrifice for Ireland. However, the implication that Lalor was a "Gaeilgeoir" is incorrect.[2] There is no evidence in any of the primary sources that Lalor wrote or spoke in Irish, or that he was even familiar with the language. On the contrary, he exhibited a lifelong passion for English literature that was stoked by his reading of authors such as Walter Scott and William Wordsworth. If this first example conveys a false impression of Lalor's cultural background, the second misrepresents his physical appearance. A large bronze sculpture of Lalor unveiled outside Portlaoise County Hall in 2007 depicts him as tall and upright, brandishing a sheaf of documents in his outstretched left arm.[3] In fact, Lalor was, according to his Young Ireland colleague, Michael Doheny, a "distorted, ill-

---

[1] The headstone was the work of the National Graves Association (NGA), a body set up during the 1920s "to save the Irish patriots' graves from oblivion" (*Irish Press*, 11 Sep. 1931). The NGA overlooked the erroneous date of birth in the inscription. Lalor was born in 1807, not 1809.
[2] An Irish speaker or Irish language enthusiast.
[3] *Irish Times*, 17 Dec. 2007.

favoured, hunch-backed little creature".[4] Other associates corroborated this description of a man whose physical appearance conflicted with the image they expected of such an inspirational writer.[5]

These misrepresentations of Lalor indicate how little importance is attached to the facts of his life, even when such details are readily available. Unfortunately, the same tendency often applies to Lalor's literary legacy. It is not that his doctrines and teachings have been deliberately misinterpreted. The problem arises from a lack of serious engagement by academia with his writings. This omission is underscored in several recent studies of Irish intellectual history, which either barely mention Lalor or ignore him completely.[6] Outside this specialist field, scholars of nineteenth-century Irish history have usually incorporated Lalor into their analyses of the period. However, setting aside the issue of his stance on property rights, these studies tend to depict Lalor as no more than a catalyst in the decision by Young Irelanders, such as John Mitchel, to take Irish nationalism in a more radical direction than heretofore. Little effort is made to investigate the theories that so entranced Mitchel and his fellow nationalists, or to explore the complexities of Lalor's relationships with them.[7]

While a definitive and comprehensive biography of James Fintan Lalor has yet to be published, that is not the object of this study. Rather the book seeks to address the historiographical lacunae and misperceptions as far as his writings are concerned. Although some biographical information is interspersed throughout the analysis that follows, the emphasis is on Lalor's efforts during the last few years of his life to reinvigorate and redirect the nationalist agenda through his access to leading figures such as Charles Gavan Duffy and the aforementioned John Mitchel.

The first chapter assesses his extant writings in considerable detail in order to clarify their meaning, especially on the land question. In this initial analysis,

---

[4] Charles Gavan Duffy, *Four Years of Irish History, 1845-1849: a Sequel to "Young Ireland"* (London, 1883), p. 478.
[5] *Irish Nation*, 3 Dec. 1881. Duffy, *Four Years of Irish History*, p. 465.
[6] Maurice Goldring, *Pleasant the Scholar's Life: Irish Intellectuals and the Construction of the Nation State* (London, 1993), p. 96. Liam O'Dowd (ed.), *On Intellectuals and Intellectual Life in Ireland: International, Comparative and Historical Contexts* (Belfast, 1996). Thomas Duddy, *A History of Irish Thought* (London, 2002), p. 289. Séamas Ó Síocháin, (ed.), *Social Thought on Ireland in the Nineteenth Century* (Dublin, 2009). Tom Boylan, Renee Prendergast and John D. Turner (eds.), *A History of Irish Economic Thought* (London, 2011), p. 99.
[7] Although scholars, such as F. S. L. Lyons (*Ireland since the Famine* (London, 1973), pp. 108-12), and R. F. Foster (*Modern Ireland 1600-1972* (London, 1989), pp. 381-2), provide insightful interpretations of these issues, the space allotted to Lalor in these lengthy historical surveys is insufficient for a full examination of his thinking.

Lalor's communication strategy, i.e. his approach to disseminating his proposals and his choice of target audience, is also examined.

In the second chapter, the possible origins of Lalor's theories are explored. While his interpretation of Irish nationalism was more radical than many of his contemporaries were prepared to accept, it would not have been out of place in the recent revolutionary past dominated by figures such as Wolfe Tone and Robert Emmet. However, his views on land tenure were far more innovative. Not only did Lalor break new ground within Irish nationalism by linking the pursuit of independence with the land question, his vision of how that question could be settled under a local administration was, in the Irish context at least, radical and subversive. The second chapter evaluates the originality or otherwise of Lalor's ideas on landholding and the rights of property by examining the writings of earlier thinkers with views similar to his own.

In the third and final chapter, the impact of Lalor's proposals on his contemporaries is examined. Lalor's audience was diverse, comprising close family members and friends, fellow nationalists whom he encountered after he entered the public arena, and the wider public who read his articles and letters. His activities were also followed closely by opponents of Irish independence, such as the British press. By analysing how Lalor's ideas were received during his lifetime, the extent of his immediate influence can be gauged.

It may be a solitary process, but researching and writing an academic work is not a solo endeavour. Mine would never have seen the light of day without the help and support of numerous people at Oxford University. These include the administrative staff at Wadham College and the History Faculty, who made my regular interactions with the university pleasant and painless. Having access to the treasures held at the Bodleian Library was a particular joy during my time at the university. However, my research took place mostly in Dublin and I spent many fruitful hours exploring the numerous primary sources safeguarded by repositories, such as the National Library and UCD Archives.

From time to time, I was fortunate to receive advice and support from a number of generous academics, especially Dr Carla King of Dublin City University. A constant source of encouragement and constructive criticism was my supervisor, Professor Marc Mulholland, to whom I am very grateful.

I would never have made it to Oxford without the grounding in history I received from the brilliant staff at Trinity College Dublin. My four years as an undergraduate student there were made possible by the education grants provided by Dun Laoghaire-Rathdown County Council. I am grateful to both TCD and the County Council for everything they did.

Finally, I could not have done any of it without my family: my wife Margaret, our wonderful sons, Alan, Stephen, and Damian, our daughters-in-law, Louise,

Dorota, and Maria, and, of course, the next generation of Bruce grandchildren: Conor, Cian, Noah, Patrick, Stella, and Adam. Their faith in me has been inspirational. Special thanks are due to Margaret, for her unstinting love and boundless common sense, and to Damian for proof-reading not only a draft of my thesis, but many other essays and papers since I returned to formal education in 2008.

To you, the reader, I offer a big thank you for your interest in James Fintan Lalor and the ideas that preoccupied him during his final years. Although I have tried to find and fix all errors and omissions in what follows, any that made it into print are entirely my responsibility and no one else's.

Chapter One

James Fintan Lalor's
"Peculiar Views on the Tenure Question"

In this opening chapter, the writings of James Fintan Lalor on the topics of nationalism and landholding in Ireland are examined in detail. The primary objective is to illuminate his proposals for a settlement of the land question in the context of the struggle for national sovereignty. In order to appreciate the position that Lalor took on these matters, it is necessary firstly to explore Irish land tenure from both theoretical and practical perspectives. As described below, the contradiction between the two contributed greatly to the increasingly fractious land question during the period in question.

Duties vs. rights: Land tenure in Ireland

The seventh edition of *The Encyclopaedia Britannica*, published between 1830 and 1842, defined Tenure as, "signify[ing] the manner in which lands or tenements are held, or the service which the tenant owes to his lord". The article went on to outline the position obtaining in the United Kingdom, where:

> ...all the lands in the kingdom are supposed to be held, mediately or immediately, of the king, who is styled the lord paramount, or above all.[1]

The status of landholders as tenants of the monarch was therefore the official legal position throughout the common law jurisdiction of Britain and Ireland. This was not merely the opinion of the *Encyclopaedia's* editors; the passage quoted was taken verbatim from the most authoritative legal text available at the time: William Blackstone's *Commentaries on the Laws of England*.[2] Blackstone further underlined the distinctive nature of English land tenure by citing the contention of an earlier English jurist, Edward Coke, that "in the law of England we have not properly *allodium*". As the same edition of the *Encyclopaedia* defined it, Allodium "denotes lands which are the absolute property of their owner, without being obliged to pay any service or acknowledgement whatever to a superior lord".[3] Legally speaking, therefore,

---

[1] *The Encyclopaedia Britannica*, 7th edn (21 vols, Edinburgh, 1842), xxi, p. 184.
[2] William Blackstone, *Commentaries on the Laws of England*, 15th edn, ed. Edward Christian, (4 vols, London, 1809), ii, p. 59.
[3] *Encyclopaedia Britannica*, ii, pp. 528-9.

even the highest-ranking English aristocrat held his land as a tenant of the king. As described below, Lalor's novel adaptation of this principle became the lynchpin of his programme for land reform.

Legal precepts that placed limitations on their property rights impinged little on the thinking of Irish landlords. Among those who noted the discrepancy between theory and practice was a French lawyer and social reformer named Gustave de Beaumont. He toured Ireland during the summer of 1837 in order to observe and report on the condition of the country and its people.[4] Beaumont characterised the British monarch's lordship over the land "as a legal fiction totally destitute of reality", with the landowner enjoying what, in effect, were "absolute" property rights.[5] In Ireland, the practical impact of this *de facto* situation was felt, not by the king, but by those of his subjects who tilled the land as occupying tenants.

The perception of a proprietor as outright owner of his land is reinforced by the comments of future Chancellor of the Exchequer, George Cornewall Lewis. In 1837 Lewis asserted that legislation to deal with Whiteboy violence against Irish landlords would "restor[e] to landowners the power of doing what they will with their own", and make them—like their English counterparts—"masters of their own property".[6] Shortly after Lewis made his comments, a number of Tipperary landlords petitioned the British government to enact legislation to curb the agrarian violence being waged against them. However, in a written response dated 22 May 1838, the under-secretary at Dublin Castle, Thomas Drummond, argued for a different approach.

Instead of seeking "the enactment or enforcement of statutes of extraordinary severity", the landlords, he wrote, should adopt a more humane approach to their tenants. Invoking the principle enunciated by Blackstone, Drummond contended that "Property has its duties as well as its rights..."[7] He was not referring directly to landholders' duties to the sovereign, but to an obligation to their tenants who risked starvation if evicted. That Drummond felt it necessary to make such a bold assertion illustrates the extent to which Irish landlords saw their land as a personal asset to be used as they wished, with little regard paid

---

[4] Tom Garvin, Andreas Hess, "Gustave de Beaumont: Ireland's Alexis de Tocqueville", in Ó Síocháin, *Social Thought on Ireland*, pp. 9-26.
[5] Gustave de Beaumont, *Ireland: Social, Political, and Religious*, ed. and tr. William Cooke Taylor (2 vols, London, 1839), ii, p. 234.
[6] George Cornewall Lewis, *Remarks on the Third Report of the Irish Poor Inquiry Commissioners* (London, 1837), p. 15.
[7] R. Barry O'Brien, *Thomas Drummond, Under-Secretary in Ireland, 1835-40; Life and Letters* (London, 1889), p. 284.

to the rights of the occupiers. This was underscored by the decision of the letter's addressees to suppress its contents, arguing that, if made public, Drummond's remark about the duties of landowners would only fuel the agrarian outrages in the country.[8]

As described in the next chapter, Beaumont's "legal fiction" was just as relevant in Britain, where landowners assumed similar rights over their landed property. However, the crucial difference lay in the treatment of tenants, which many commentators believed was uniquely harsh in Ireland.[9] One of these observers was Alexander Somerville, an English journalist who, towards the end of 1843, published a pamphlet in which he described a particularly egregious case of landlord persecution of his tenants.[10] According to Somerville's account, a Kilkenny-based landlord named Richard Shee instigated protracted legal proceedings against several of his tenants who were otherwise protected by their leases. Shee's aim, according to the pamphlet, was to drain the tenants' finances by compelling them to incur prohibitive legal costs, thus enabling him to evict them for non-payment of rent. Somerville's pamphlet was brought to the attention of the leader of the Whig opposition, Lord John Russell, and the Conservative Prime Minister, Sir Robert Peel.[11] Both men expressed their dismay in the House of Commons. Russell declared that "some landlords are exercising a fearful and dreadful power in Ireland".[12] The Prime Minister expressed his shock "at the manner in which the legal powers of the landlords are too frequently used in Ireland". However, he saw no point in bringing in legislation to curb these powers until "the whole state of the relations of landlords and tenants in Ireland should be ascertained and made clear". This would require a commission which the government had just set up under the chairmanship of William Courtenay, tenth earl of Devon.[13]

In their report published in February 1845, the earl of Devon and his four colleagues found that the tenure system in Ireland had evolved quite differently

---

[8] Ibid., pp. 287-8.
[9] See, for instance, Arthur Young, *A Tour in Ireland* (2 vols, Dublin, 1780), ii, Part II, pp. 40-1. James Ebenezer Bicheno, *Ireland and its Economy: Being the Result of Observations Made in a Tour Through the Country in 1829* (London, 1830), p. 159. Frederick von Raumer, *England in 1835: Being a series of letters written to friends in Germany*, tr. Sarah Austin and H. E. Lloyd (3 vols, London, 1836), iii, pp. 189-92.
[10] Alexander Somerville, *A Cry from Ireland, or, Landlord and tenant exemplified* (London, 1843). The pamphlet was published anonymously as the author feared being sued for libel. (See idem, *The Whistler at the Plough* (Manchester, 1852), pp. 454-5).
[11] Idem, *Whistler at the Plough*, p. 455.
[12] [Hansard], *Parliamentary Debates*, vol. 72, col. 722 (13 Feb. 1844).
[13] *Parl. Debs.*, vol. 73, col. 237-8 (23 Feb. 1844).

to that of Britain, leading to poor relations between landlords and tenants.[14] For a number of historic factors—principally the sixteenth-century Reformation, the Cromwellian and Williamite land seizures a century later, and the imposition of the Penal Laws in the early 1700s—the land of Ireland was owned by a relatively small number of mainly Protestant landlords, while the bulk of the tenantry who worked the land were Catholic. As O'Neill put it in an article on the land question during the first half of the nineteenth century; "There was no bond of sympathy between landlord and tenant—they differed in race, religion and tradition".[15] This cultural divide favoured the landlord, and tenants were vulnerable to arbitrary rent increases and summary eviction. With no political option available to aggrieved tenants, some turned to violence against landlords deemed guilty of unjust treatment.[16]

Although set up to recommend how tensions over Irish land could be reduced if not resolved, the Devon Commission was constituted so as to prevent any serious dilution of landlord interests. Its stated objectives were:

> to suggest amendments in the laws which, having due regard to the rights of property, may appear calculated to encourage the cultivation of the soil, to extend a better system of agriculture, and to improve the relation between landlord and tenant.[17]

The inviolable status afforded to "the rights of property" made it unlikely that the commission was interested in radical reform, especially as it was composed entirely of landlords.[18] The commission conducted interviews around the country and, having considered its findings, found that "the larger proportion of the land is occupied by tenants-at-will... [due to] ...an indisposition in many landlords to grant leases..."[19] Nevertheless, they did not recommend any legislative intervention to correct this. Instead, they felt, possible solutions should be left to "the discretion of individuals".[20] In short, if a tenant were to achieve security of tenure he would have to negotiate directly with his landlord.

---

[14] *Parliamentary Papers* (1845), XXVIII. [1], Report from Her Majesty's Commissioners of inquiry into the state of the Law and Practice in respect to the Occupation of Land in Ireland, pp. 6-7.
[15] Thomas Patrick O'Neill, "The Irish Land Question, 1830-1850", *Studies*, 44/175, Aug. 1955, p. 325.
[16] Ibid., pp. 325-7.
[17] *The Times*, 4 Dec. 1843.
[18] *Parl. Debs.*, vol. 73, col. 237-8 (23 Feb. 1844). Daniel O'Connell compared the commission to "a board of foxes gravely deliberating over a flock of geese". (*The Times*, 20 Dec. 1843).
[19] *Parl. Paps.* (1845), XXVIII. [1], p. 15.
[20] Ibid.

However, as the Shee case illustrated, even the existence of a lease did not necessarily prevent a landowner from dispossessing a tenant. Seven months after publication of the Devon Commission report, Irish newspapers were reporting the arrival of potato blight and the prospect of famine.[21] The still-unresolved conflict between landlords and tenants was about to reach a new level of intensity as starvation and disease gripped the countryside.

James Fintan Lalor: Background

One of the witnesses interviewed at the Devon Commission's hearings was Patrick ('Patt') Lalor (1781-1856), a prosperous tenant farmer who held 1,000 acres in Queen's County (now County Laois), some of which he let to sub-tenants.[22] Lalor was a prominent supporter of Daniel O'Connell and served as a member of parliament for several years during the early 1830s.[23] Between April 1847 and July 1848, his eldest son, James Fintan, had 10 letters and articles published in the national press. Apart from a few letters to provincial papers, these writings constitute the younger Lalor's only known published work. In them, he outlined a number of radical proposals to reform land tenure in famine-stricken Ireland. It is for his bold policy of linking independence and land reform, encapsulated in the memorable phrase, "like a railway carriage to the engine", that he is probably best remembered today.[24] For many years, following his death on 27 December 1849 at the age of 42, Lalor and his ideas were largely forgotten. However, during the latter part of the century, he was rediscovered by a new generation of nationalists, mainly through the advocacy of old associates, such as Thomas Luby and Charles Gavan Duffy. Following the republication of Lalor's newspaper articles in 1895, he became elevated to the status of a "nationalist prophet" whose writings on the major social, economic and political themes of his day seemed almost timeless.[25] This quality ensured

---

[21] *Freeman's Journal*, 17 Sep. 1845.
[22] Thomas Patrick O'Neill, *James Fintan Lalor*, tr. John T. Goulding (Wexford, 2003), p. 21.
[23] Bridget Hourican, "Lalor, Patrick ('Patt')", *DIB* (Cambridge, 2009), (http://dib.cambridge.org/viewReadPage.do?articleId=a4646) 30 Mar. 2017.
[24] *Irish Felon*, 1 Jul. 1848. (Lalor, James Fintan, *"The Faith of a Felon" and other writings*, ed. Marta Ramón (Dublin, 2012), p. 126.)
[25] T. G. O'Donoghue (ed.), *The Writings of James Fintan Lalor, with an introduction embodying personal recollections by John O'Leary, and a brief memoir* (Dublin, 1895). Subsequent collections include Nathaniel Marlowe (ed.), *Collected Writings of James Fintan Lalor* (Dublin, 1918). Eva Guarino and Judith Turnbull (eds.), *Collected Writings by and about James Fintan Lalor* (Rome, 1999).

that, for figures as different in their political and cultural outlooks as Patrick Pearse and James Connolly, Lalor's thinking was both relevant and inspiring.[26]

While Lalor's writings have been an enduring source of inspiration, details of his life are sketchy. He had just turned 40 years old when his first article was published and he seems to have spent most of his life up to that point living in relative obscurity at the family home at Tinakill, near Abbeyleix. He suffered from lifelong chronic bronchitis caused by a childhood injury that left him with a spinal deformity, and this undoubtedly contributed to his relatively sheltered upbringing.[27] Significant gaps in the historical record are reflected in the small secondary literature, most of which comprises articles and essays introducing collections of his writings. There are only two book-length biographies available in English and these were published as recently as 1990 and 2003 respectively.[28] The fact that the two authors managed to produce not much more than 100 pages of original content each indicates how little material they had to work with. Of course, Lalor's relatively short life, a tiny fraction of which was spent in the public eye, is a contributory factor. He did not live long enough to develop and refine his thinking or to fashion his own image for posterity, as so many of his contemporaries did.[29] A further blow to scholarly research is that Lalor led quite a peripatetic life in his last years after he attracted the attention of the police. So although he exhibited an almost lawyerly regard for documentary evidence, from time to time, he was compelled to entrust his papers to others and, following his death, many of these were lost. Apart from that, the sometimes seditious content of his letters led some of his correspondents to burn them as soon as they were read.[30] Other material was confiscated and presumably destroyed when the offices of *The Irish Felon*, to which Lalor contributed his last articles, were raided by the authorities.

Academia and Lalor

While the original newspaper articles represent the main source for the present analysis, a true appreciation of their contents is difficult without also consulting

---

[26] Christine Kinealy, *Repeal and Revolution: 1848 in Ireland* (Oxford, 2009), p. 284.
[27] Mary E. Daly, "Lalor, James Fintan", *DIB*, (Cambridge, 2009), (http://dib.cambridge.org/viewReadPage.do?articleId=a4646) 30 Mar. 2017.
[28] David N. Buckley, *James Fintan Lalor: Radical* (Cork, 1990). Thomas Patrick O'Neill, *James Fintan Lalor* (Wexford, 2003). The latter book is a translation of Tomás Ó Néill's, *Fiontán Ó Leathlobhair*, an Irish-language biography published in 1962. As Thomas P. O'Neill, the author has also written numerous articles in English on various aspects of Lalor's life and work.
[29] James Quinn, *Young Ireland and the Writing of Irish History* (Dublin, 2015), pp. 100-17.
[30] Thomas Patrick O'Neill, "The papers of James Fintan Lalor in the National Library", *Irish Book Lover*, 30/4, January 1948, pp. 84-86.

the surviving archive of manuscript material. This material comprises those letters, draft articles, notes, etc., which belonged to Lalor, his family, and his close associates. These documents shed light on Lalor's communications strategy and on his relations with his putative allies in the Young Ireland movement. They also help the researcher to make sense of the apparent inconsistencies and contradictions that arise from a reading of the published articles. By examining those articles in conjunction with the manuscripts, it is possible to clear up a point of confusion that has bedevilled the modern Lalor historiography. Scholars are unable to agree on whether he was a proponent of land nationalisation, i.e. state ownership or control of the land, or an advocate of peasant proprietorship whereby tenants would gain legal title to their holdings from the current landlords.

Examples of these differences can be found in two well-known reference works on Ireland:

> [Lalor] advocated land nationalisation, believing that the entire soil of a country belongs of right to the entire people and is the rightful property not of any one class but of the nation at large; he probably influenced Marx, who asserted that monopoly, is the basis of monopoly in capital.[31]

> Lalor was later appropriated by James Connolly and Patrick Pearse as the forerunner of socialist republicanism, although his objective of peasant proprietorship fell short of real agrarian socialism.[32]

As these extracts indicate, the authors were not in agreement on the system of landholding which Lalor was championing, i.e., land nationalisation versus peasant proprietorship. These "summary judgements" are derived from nearly a century of academic debate about Lalor, his role within Young Ireland, and his teachings on land tenure. Before proceeding with a fresh exploration of the primary sources, it is necessary to analyse the Lalor historiography in order to understand how and why academic confusion and dissension have developed.

Lillian Fogarty's collection of Lalor's writings published in 1918 is deemed to mark the beginning of Lalor scholarship.[33] As well as comprising transcripts of Lalor's published articles in *The Nation* and *The Irish Felon*, Fogarty's book included a selection of private correspondence between Lalor and others,

---

[31] Marjorie Bloy, "Lalor, James Fintan", in Brian Lalor, ed., *Encyclopaedia of Ireland* (Dublin, 2003), p. 604.
[32] Peter Gray, "Lalor, James Fintan", in Sean J. Connolly (ed.), *Oxford Companion to Irish History*, 2nd ed., (Oxford, 2002), p. 294.
[33] O'Neill, *JFL*, p. 15. Buckley, *JFL*, p. 8.

notably his brother Richard and the nationalist leader, John Mitchel.[34] Little is known about Fogarty's background. She was not a trained historian, having graduated from UCD in 1917 with a degree in Irish and French.[35] This may explain why none of the biographical information about Lalor in Fogarty's introduction is supported by any documentary sources. She seems to have drawn mainly from oral evidence passed on by descendants of Lalor's associates — an example of what she referred to as Ireland's "unwritten history".[36] The most contentious assertion in Fogarty's essay is that Lalor visited France twice, firstly around the time of the July Revolution of 1830, and later during the February Revolution of 1848.[37] The absence of any documentary corroboration for Lalor's French sojourns has led later historians to dismiss the claims.[38] Nevertheless, since its publication more than a century ago, Fogarty's book has been a frequent source for researchers and academics discussing Lalor and his times.[39] Although she was sympathetic to the view that Lalor might have been a proto-land nationaliser, Fogarty stopped short of an unequivocal statement to that effect.[40]

The availability of some of Lalor's private papers in 1926 opened up the potential for a deeper understanding of his views on the land question. Fogarty was among the first researchers to explore this new material. In 1947 she published a revised edition of her Lalor collection, incorporating an updated introduction.[41] Lalor soon found a new interpreter in the form of historian and archivist, Thomas P. O'Neill. Between 1948 and 1962, O'Neill produced a number of mostly article-length studies of Lalor and the land question during the early nineteenth century, culminating in his Irish-language biography of the reformer. Through his work as an official at the National Library of Ireland, O'Neill had easy access to the archival material held there and published a

---

[34] Lillian Fogarty, *James Fintan Lalor: Patriot and Political Essayist (1807-1849), with a preface by Arthur Griffith* (Dublin, 1918).
[35] UCD, *Calendar 1918-1919* (Dublin, 1919), p. 861.
[36] Fogarty, *JFL*, p. xxiii.
[37] Ibid., pp. xxi, xxviii.
[38] e.g. Buckley, *JFL*, pp. 15-6.
[39] Among the many historical studies referencing Fogarty's collection are: Lyons, *Ireland since the Famine*, Foster, *Modern Ireland*, K. Theodore Hoppen, *Ireland since 1800: Conflict and Conformity* (Harlow, 1999), D. George Boyce, *Nineteenth Century Ireland: the Search for Stability*, 2nd edn (Dublin, 2005). It remains to be seen whether Ramón's Lalor collection will replace Fogarty as the standard reference.
[40] Fogarty, *JFL*, pp. xxxix.
[41] Lillian Fogarty, *James Fintan Lalor: Patriot and Political Essayist - Collected Writings, with a biographical note by L. Fogarty, M. A. (Bean T. Uí Thuama)* (Dublin, 1947), p. xlvii.

short guide to the Lalor papers in 1948.[42] O'Neill remains unsurpassed in terms of Lalor scholarship and, despite expressing some misgivings, historians regard his biography as the standard work on its subject.[43] In an article published in 1950, O'Neill conducted the first detailed analysis of Lalor's economic thinking as expressed in *The Nation* and *The Irish Felon* articles.[44] In his discussion of Lalor's views on the land question, O'Neill concluded that, despite his apparent support for "the abolition of all private property", Lalor actually upheld the rights of the individual landowner.[45] O'Neill argued that Lalor saw "the general right of the people as first proprietors" as a theoretical entitlement only. This was because, he contended, Lalor also envisaged that once the land was redistributed more equitably, "the majority of people [would have] a durable interest in its maintenance".[46] In other words, according to O'Neill, Lalor favoured the transfer of ownership of the land from the existing landlords to their occupying tenants. (This, of course, was the basis of the settlement enacted by the British government several decades after Lalor's death.)

Given O'Neill's knowledge of Lalor and his writings, his argument that Lalor was not a land nationaliser deserves further consideration. However, it quickly becomes clear that O'Neill was keen to distance his subject from any association with atheistic communism. What he saw as the appropriation of his ideas by some "Marxist historians" placed Lalor "under a cloud". Accordingly, O'Neill began his article with a stout defence of his subject's religious credentials. This was designed to dispel doubts "in the popular mind" that Lalor was anything but a loyal son of the Catholic Church.[47] Later, in the biography, O'Neill linked Michael Davitt's teaching that "the land was directly the possession of the state" with the rise of fascist and communist regimes in the first half of the twentieth century. Moreover Davitt's concept, he asserted, was one that Lalor would never have dreamt of.[48] The possibility that not all proponents of land nationalisation were either socialists or fascists does not

---

[42] O'Neill, "Papers of James Fintan Lalor", pp. 84-6.
[43] Carla King, "Radical activist: review of James Fintan Lalor by Thomas P. O'Neill", *Books Ireland*, No. 270, Oct., 2004, pp.. 231-2. Patrick Maume, "O'Neill, Thomas Patrick", *DIB* (Cambridge, 2009), (http://dib.cambridge.org/viewReadPage.do?articleId=a6941) 15 Feb. 2017.
[44] Thomas Patrick O'Neill, "The economic and political ideas of James Fintan Lalor", *Irish Ecclesiastical Record*, 74/ , 1950, pp. 398-409. O'Neill incorporated much of the content of this article into his later biography of Lalor.
[45] Ibid., p. 402.
[46] Ibid., p. 403.
[47] Ibid, p. 398.
[48] O'Neill, *JFL*, p. 120.

seem to have occurred to O'Neill, and he made no attempt to examine the principles involved as set out in the writings of Henry George, for instance.[49] Consequently, despite O'Neill's evident scholarship, his focus on Lalor within the comparatively narrow context of Irish nationalism and the Irish land question, and his unwillingness to resist the religious and political mores of the time, tend to undermine his case.

Between 1990 and the publication in 2003 of O'Neill's biography in translation, Buckley's was the only book-length study of Lalor in English. The author devoted most of his short book to an analysis of Lalor's thinking on various subjects, including the land question. The biographical element came a distant second to Buckley's aim of addressing what he termed "the central dilemma of Lalor's career: viz, whether he was a Nationalist or a Socialist".[50] Buckley's goal was laudable, i.e. to "rescue" Lalor from those later admirers who, in his colourful phrase, regarded him as a "prophet" whom they were attempting to "press-gang into service and subservience… [to] the 'party' line".[51] While Buckley's attempt to delve more deeply than other scholars into Lalor's thinking is commendable, his contribution to the historiography is, according to one reviewer, "directionless and idiosyncratic".[52] This is evident in his rather cynical depiction of Lalor as "hawking his ideas about from post to pillar", and in the surprisingly superficial understanding of his subject's teachings that Buckley exhibits, particularly in relation to the land question.[53] Without adequate explanation, Buckley characterised Foster's assertion that Lalor was "an advocate of land nationalisation" as a "common misinterpretation".[54] Yet, in his discussion of Lalor's proposal that landholders would pay rent to the state rather than to private landlords, he seemed unaware of its similarity to George's teaching that "rent, the creation of the whole community, necessarily belongs to the whole community".[55] Perhaps Buckley's determination to pin an ideological label on Lalor indicated an inability or unwillingness on his part to grasp the full radical nature of his subject's ideas on landholding.

Outside the realm of these "Lalor specialists', leading historians have tended to depict him as an influential but ultimately marginal figure during the rise and fall of Young Ireland in the late-1840s. His brief career as a revolutionary is

---

[49] Henry George, *Progress and Poverty* (New York. 5th edition, 1881).
[50] Buckley, *JFL*, p. 8.
[51] Ibid., p. 5.
[52] James Kelly, "Review: James Fintan Lalor: Radical by David N. Buckley", *Studia Hibernica*, No. 26, 1992, pp. 255-7.
[53] Buckley, *JFL*, p. 28.
[54] Ibid., p. 37, fn.42. Foster, *Modern Ireland*, p. 314, fn. xxiv.
[55] Buckley, *JFL*, p. 64. George, *Progress and Poverty*, p. 328.

generally dismissed as inconsequential. For Foster, Lalor's attempted "rising in 1849 was a mere hiccough".[56] Lee barely mentioned Lalor in his study of Irish history since the Famine, referring only to his stillborn revolt as having "failed so farcically".[57] It is for his role as an *éminence grise* that Lalor has received more scholarly attention. Hoppen portrayed Lalor as an ally to John Mitchel, as the latter became increasingly militant towards the end of 1847.[58] Although Foster touched briefly on the influence that Lalor exerted through his ideas on land reform, a fuller, more nuanced, analysis of Lalor's contribution is to be found in F. S. L. Lyons' synthesis of post-Famine Irish history.[59] Lyons characterised Lalor's philosophy as "fragmentary, hasty and ill-considered", but he also acknowledged his influence, not only on Mitchel, but on later activists such as Michael Davitt and Patrick Pearse. [60] Lyons played down any radical interpretation of Lalor's ideas on land tenure, disagreeing with the proposition that Lalor was "against private property in land".[61] Foster, on the other hand, wrote of Lalor "urging land nationalization", a virtually unheard of concept in 1840s Ireland.[62] Apart from Diarmuid Ferriter, who also associated Lalor with land nationalisation, most historians who addressed this aspect of Lalor's thinking have agreed with Lyons' more conservative analysis.[63] Lalor's status as a minor character in Irish historiography is perhaps best illustrated by his inclusion in a collection of articles on the theme of notable figures who failed to achieve their stated objectives.[64] The author of the well-researched article on Lalor, Mary E. Daly, highlighted the contradiction between the successive failures of his short public career, and his posthumous influence on both the Land League strategy of 1879, and Pearse's commitment to military action in 1916. In short, Daly argued that Lalor's legacy rests on his writings and not on his activism. Yet, notwithstanding her perceptive insight that Lalor's initial declarations on land were "obscure and open to numerous interpretations", she rejected any implication that Lalor was a socialist, concluding that all he was proposing was "either tenant right, or peasant ownership of land, nothing more radical".[65]

---

[56] Foster, *Modern Ireland*, p. 382.
[57] J. J. Lee, *The Modernisation of Irish Society 1848-1918* (Dublin, 2008), p. 37.
[58] Hoppen, *Ireland since 1800*, p. 34.
[59] Lyons, *Ireland since the Famine*, pp. 108-12.
[60] Ibid., p. 111.
[61] Ibid., p. 108.
[62] Foster, *Modern Ireland*, p. 314, fn. xxiv.
[63] Diarmaid Ferriter, *The Transformation of Ireland 1900-2000* (London, 2005), p. 547.
[64] Mary E. Daly, "James Fintan Lalor (1807-1849) and rural revolution" in Ciaran Brady (ed.), *Worsted in the Game: Losers in Irish History* (Dublin, 1989), pp. 111-19.
[65] Ibid., pp. 115-6.

This brief review of the secondary literature underlines the lack of any detailed scholarly exploration of Lalor's position on the land question. In light of the peripheral role Lalor played in the already minor revolutionary activities of 1848 and 1849, it is not too difficult to understand why he has been largely side-lined in the general historiography of the period. Moreover, academic interest in the Irish land question of the nineteenth century has tended to concentrate on two key areas: agitation in Ireland for tenant rights, and British government attempts to respond through increasingly radical legislation. The rather esoteric image associated with communal ownership of land, especially in Ireland where individual land ownership has traditionally been so prized, has probably also been a factor in deterring serious historical investigation of Lalor's ideas. Finally, for much of the twentieth century, the issue of land nationalisation was tainted by association with socialism, not a belief system easily reconciled by some with the views of a revered nationalist such as James Fintan Lalor. Speculation about scholarly motivation must yield, however, to a key finding of this literature review. None of the historians discussed offered any detailed arguments in support of his or her position on Lalor's land policy, i.e. nationaliser or upholder of peasant proprietorship. What is more, no serious attempt has been made to examine Lalor's landholding proposals outside the Irish nationalist framework. For instance, his writings have not been studied in the context of eighteenth- and nineteenth-century social or economic commentary on land tenure, let alone the radical propositions put forward by reformers such as William Ogilvie, Thomas Spence or James 'Bronterre' O'Brien. Finally, the secondary literature has failed to acknowledge the evolving nature of either Lalor's thinking or of his communications strategy once he had formulated his principles. Both of these are crucial to any understanding of his published writings, as will become clear in this and subsequent chapters.

Lalor's early writings

A central argument of this chapter is that the advent of the potato blight in 1845 was pivotal in the formation of Lalor's ideas on landholding. The impact of the resulting Famine on his thinking can be gauged from an examination of the small number of his writings that pre-date its arrival. These earlier sources reveal a cast of mind that was conventional and supportive of the establishment—far removed from the radical perspectives he displayed a few years later. In the summer of 1843, Lalor wrote to the British Prime Minister, Sir Robert Peel. This letter was preserved in the British Museum and discovered by Thomas O'Neill in 1952.[66] In the letter, Lalor expressed his belief that "it is only

---

[66] JFL to Sir Robert Peel, Jun. 1843, NLI, Ms. 18,390 (photocopy of original).

to a Conservative Government, to her landed proprietors, and to *peace*, that this country can look for any improvement in her social condition". What is more, he indicated that he would soon join the Conservative party himself. His primary reason for writing was to offer his services to the government as a source of inside information about the Repeal Association, a movement which he hoped would be "speedily and safely suppressed… fully and for ever". His credentials were sound. He described how the involvement of his close relatives, including his father, in the association gave him unique insights into their activities and plans. Lalor's letter aroused considerable interest in government circles and further letters were exchanged. However, there is no evidence that Peel took up Lalor's offer and the correspondence ended.[67] Still determined to make some impact on Irish affairs, Lalor turned to the second of the two authorities he had invoked in his letter to Peel: Ireland's landowners. In January 1844 he wrote a letter, seemingly intended for publication, entitled "To the landowners of Ireland on the aims of an Irish Agricultural Society". Apparently, this was to be the first of a series in which Lalor addressed Irish landlords as the source "of any real and rational hope" for a better future for Ireland and its people. The memory of having been rebuffed by the Conservatives was clearly still fresh in his mind.

> It is most unwise and unjust to be looking ever and altogether to Government… Government can do much; but there are things which Government cannot do; which men must do for themselves, or have undone.[68]

The letter does not seem to have made it into print and less than 20 pages survive from what was at least a 47-page document.

Scholars have speculated about the possible reasons for these offers of support to the British government and the landed gentry, both of which Lalor subsequently opposed.[69] Whether his letters were motivated by social altruism, or political cynicism, or whether they were a symptom of longstanding relationship difficulties between him and his father, cannot be determined. However, nowhere do the primary sources indicate that Lalor ever sought personal gain or advantage through the dissemination of his writings, whether private or public. Indeed his stance on the major political issues of the day, i.e. repeal and the land question, cost him his position as heir to his father's substantial property. According to O'Neill, tensions between father and son

---

[67] O'Neill, *JFL*, pp. 36-42.
[68] NLI, Ms. 340/59.
[69] Buckley, *JFL*, pp. 43, 28.

were exacerbated by the second of the letters discussed above, causing Lalor to leave home for the next two years. During this period, he lived in Dublin and Belfast.[70] Although severe illness forced James Fintan to return to Tinakill in the spring of 1846, he and his father were never truly reconciled.[71]

Lalor and the Irish Confederation

During Lalor's two-year absence potato blight had arrived in Ireland and the subsequent famine had a profound effect on his thinking about the land question. Nevertheless, he did not display any desire to publicly lead a movement to promote his new ideas and put them into practical effect. As his earlier appeals to the British government and the Irish landowners demonstrated, he preferred to exert influence on those he saw as best placed to take the country in the direction he favoured. Fobbed off by the British government and dismayed by the landowners' lack of response to the Famine, he began to see some potential in a dispute then brewing within the Repeal Association. That organisation's policies were delineated in a manifesto delivered by Daniel O'Connell to his followers in Dublin on 6 June 1843.[72] According to contemporary press reports, O'Connell reiterated the principal aim of the association as the restoration of the Irish parliament abolished by the Acts of Union of 1800. Among his other objectives was a reframing of the laws governing landlord/tenant relations, the effect of which would be to codify and extend the so-called "Ulster Custom" (also known as "tenant right") to the rest of the island. As the name suggests, tenant farmers in that province received more favourable treatment than their counterparts elsewhere in the country. Although not enshrined in law, the Ulster Custom provided security of tenure as long as the tenant paid his rent. In the event of his leaving the property for whatever reason, he could also "sell" the good will he had accumulated in the land to the incoming tenant.[73] The landlord would, of course, remain secure in the ownership of his property because, as O'Connell put it,

> nothing could have a worse effect on the prosperity of the Irish nation than to check the natural inclination men have to possess wealth in its most agreeable form—that of landed property. [74]

---

[70] O'Neill, *JFL*, pp. 43-6.

[71] Lalor died in Dublin and was buried, not in the family vault at Tinakill, but in an unmarked grave in Glasnevin Cemetery, suggesting that the rift between father and son was never mended.

[72] *Freeman's Journal*, 7 Jun. 1843. *Nation*, 10 Jun. 1843.

[73] William Neilson Hancock, *The Tenant-Right of Ulster, considered economically: being an essay read before the Dublin University Philosophical Society* (Dublin, 1845), p. 7.

[74] *Freeman's Journal*, 7 Jun. 1843. *Nation*, 10 Jun. 1843.

The backing of the landlord class was critical to the strategy of the Repeal Association, which wanted the broadest possible national support for its goals. That included the landowning aristocracy.[75] Lalor opposed O'Connell's strategy, but he was hopeful about the Young Ireland faction within the Repeal Association. As the name indicated, they were mostly in their twenties and thirties, more than a generation removed from "Old Ireland" typified by O'Connell himself who was in his late sixties when he unveiled his manifesto. By the summer of 1846 increasing tensions and a number of policy differences led to Young Ireland seceding from the association. In January they formed their own organisation to be known as the Irish Confederation.[76]

Following his return to Tinakill, Lalor kept up with these developments as they were reported in the press. By November 1846 he was contemplating joining the breakaway group although, as he confided to his friend, John Marnell, he "fear[ed] their imbecility".[77] When it became clear that the Young Irelanders would form a separate association, Lalor made his move. In January he wrote to Charles Gavan Duffy (1816-1903), a leading Young Irelander and soon to be a member of the Irish Confederation's ruling council.[78] Lalor offered his support to the new body—if it agreed not to adopt any resolutions committing it to repeal of the Act of Union by legal means only. In his letter, Lalor also urged Duffy to consider the land question as being of much greater significance than repeal.[79] By the time Duffy replied to his letter, a report of the new Confederation's inaugural meeting had appeared in *The Nation*. This would have made it clear to Lalor that his suggestions had not been heeded. Although supposedly of a more radical hue than their parent body, Young Ireland shared similar objectives and principles. At the Confederation's first gathering in Dublin, its new leader, William Smith O'Brien, reiterated his public pledge from several years earlier to seek "the Repeal of the Union with England by all peaceable, moral, and constitutional means..."[80] He addressed an ecstatic crowd at the inaugural meeting in terms that would not have elicited any dissent from Daniel O'Connell:

---

[75] Lawrence J. McCaffrey, *Daniel O'Connell and the Repeal Year* (Kentucky, 1966), p. 81.
[76] Lyons, *Ireland since the Famine*, pp. 104-7.
[77] Marnell to JFL, 6 Nov. 1846, NLI, Ms. 340/119.
[78] *Nation*, 16 Jan. 1847.
[79] JFL to Duffy, 11 Jan. 1847, RIA 12.P.15/6. The earliest printed version is to be found in Duffy, *Four Years of Irish History*, pp. 466-70. Lalor's draft is held in the NLI, Ms 340/50.
[80] *Nation*, 16 Jan. 1847.

> Repeal cannot be carried by the democracy alone, nor by the aristocracy alone; but it can be carried by the combination of the nobles, gentry, and the people of Ireland, and carried without one moment's struggle.[81]

In his reply to Lalor, Duffy made it clear that the Confederation would proceed with the policies and resolutions already approved at its first meeting. However, he also complimented Lalor's "vigour of intellect" and encouraged him to join the new body's governing council where he could argue his point of view with the other members. Duffy closed his letter with a plea calculated to prick Lalor's conscience: "If you have been inactive hitherto you have a long arrear due to poor old Ireland, and ought to plunge into work."[82]

Lalor quickly overcame any disappointment he felt at the failure of his first attempt to influence the direction of the new breakaway group. He seized on the opening offered by Duffy with a much longer letter sent at the end of January.[83] In it he expanded his views on land reform and self-government, urging the Confederation to link the two, "like a railway carriage to the engine". Above all, he stressed an urgent need for concrete action before the Famine wiped out the mass of tillage farmers who possessed "the only weapon… that could conquer or cow the English government". Lalor only implied what that weapon was, but Duffy understood him to be advocating a rent-strike.[84] Following this exchange, it must have been evident to both men that a gulf existed between the radical Lalor and the moderate Confederation. Yet, as Duffy recalled later, he was sufficiently intrigued by the "freshness and force" of Lalor's writing to invite his previously unknown correspondent into the upper echelons of the Confederation.[85] For his part, Lalor recognised the public esteem in which Duffy and his colleagues were held, and hoped that through them he could further his own agenda. As he wrote in his second letter, "Men have given to you their faith, and hearts, and hopes, for your bold bearing and bold words".[86] So Lalor offered to back the Confederation's policy of enticing the landlords to support repeal, as long as they, the landlords, agreed to grant security of tenure to their tenants. However, Lalor was sceptical that the landlords would ever do so. Therefore, given

---

[81] Ibid.
[82] Duffy to JFL, undated, NLI Ms. 340/37. Probably written on 19 Jan., i.e. shortly after the inaugural meeting of the Irish Confederation held on 13 Jan,.
[83] Lalor published this letter in *The Irish Felon* (1 Jul. 1848) under the title, "To the Confederate and Repeal Clubs in Ireland". Lalor's handwritten draft is held in the NLI (Ms. 340/49).
[84] Duffy, *Four Years of Irish History*, p. 475.
[85] Ibid., p. 466.
[86] *Irish Felon*, 1 Jul. 1848. (Ramón, *JFL*, p. 125.)

the prospect of the blight reappearing in the autumn, he insisted that his support would last only "until the first day of September next".[87] In the meantime, he asked Duffy to show his letter to his colleagues in the Confederation. Two of them, Thomas D'Arcy McGee and John Mitchel, engaged in further correspondence with Lalor.[88] In March, McGee conveyed an invitation from Duffy to "re-write your letters" for publication in *The Nation*.[89]

The *Nation* articles

Together with Thomas Davis and John Blake Dillon, Duffy launched *The Nation* in 1842 as a weekly medium for nationalist-orientated news and opinion. As the most experienced newspaperman, Duffy became the editor. It was popular from the start, easily outselling its rivals and reaching a huge audience throughout the country.[90] Following the secession from the Repeal Association, the paper now supported the Young Irelanders and the Irish Confederation[91] Out of loyalty to O'Connell, Patt Lalor stopped taking *The Nation*, a significant blow to his eldest son who read it avidly each week. The latter managed to get round his father's decision by persuading his friend John Marnell to send him copies of the paper in the post.[92] Now he was being given space in Ireland's biggest-selling newspaper to articulate his ideas and argue his opinions.

Lalor based his first article on the unpublished letter "to the landowners of Ireland" written three years earlier.[93] He updated it to take account of the Famine, but otherwise, he conformed to Confederation policy by adopting what he referred to as "a lower tone".[94] Indeed, compared with his articles published a year later in *The Irish Felon*, Lalor's contributions to *The Nation* were relatively mild. Arising from his tacit agreement with Duffy, Lalor tried not to alienate a mass readership that supported repeal by revealing his unvarnished views on Ireland's relationship with Britain. Nor would he alarm the landlords by outlining his true thinking on the question of land tenure. However, he was not so circumspect in his correspondence with the

---

[87] Ibid. (Ramón, *JFL*, p. 121.)
[88] David Wilson, *Thomas D'Arcy McGee: Passion, Reason, and Politics, 1825-1857*, vol. 1 (Montreal, 2008), p. 150.
[89] McGee to JFL, 8 Mar. 1847, NLI, Ms. 340/108.
[90] Quinn, *Young Ireland*, pp. 15-7.
[91] Ann Andrews, *Newspapers and Newsmakers: the Dublin Nationalist Press in the Mid-Nineteenth Century* (Liverpool, 2014), p. 104.
[92] O'Neill, *JFL*, pp. 48-9, 66.
[93] Buckley, *JFL*, p. 17, fn. 47.
[94] JFL to Duffy, 18 Apr. 1847, NLI, Ms. 5757/25.

Confederation leaders. As Duffy reported later, "Lalor's public letters were tame compared to his private exhortations and remonstrances".[95] The importance of those private letters cannot be overstated. They underline Lalor's strategy of winning support for his position from prominent nationalist figures who, in his eyes, were in a better position than he was to lead Ireland in the direction he wished to see it take. The quid pro quo, it seems, is that Lalor would articulate Confederation policy—in his own terms—through the articles published in *The Nation*.[96] These articles represented what Lalor regarded as an "experiment" designed to persuade the landowners that they should join with the people in reconstructing the country.[97] Although *The Nation* articles only hinted at Lalor's ideas on land and repeal, they provide some context for both his private and later public exposition of those views. Therefore, before discussing the private correspondence between Lalor and the Confederation, it is worthwhile examining the published articles in some detail.

The prospect of continuing famine was uppermost in Lalor's mind when he began his contacts with the Confederation. This explains the sense of urgency that permeates his *Nation* articles. For Lalor, the Famine offered both threat and opportunity. The threat was short-term, the opportunity long-term. Both needed to be addressed if Ireland was to become the kind of society Lalor envisaged. As Ramón has pointed out, Lalor feared that the grain harvest in the autumn of 1847 would be seized by landlords to cover rent payments. This would leave smallholders facing another year of starvation if the potato crop failed again.[98] So when he wrote to Gavan Duffy in January, Lalor believed that a solution was urgently needed if a total disaster were to be avoided. As he revealed a year later:

> I was biding my time when the potato failure hurried a crisis. The landlords and English government took instant advantage of the famine, and the small occupiers began to quit in thousands. I saw that Ireland was to be won at once or lost for ever.[99]

---

[95] Duffy, *Four Years of Irish History*, p. 474.
[96] Following publication of Lalor's first article on 24 April, *The Nation* announced in the following week's edition that "Mr. James Lalor's second Letter to the Landlords will be published next week". However this did not happen and Lalor's text remained in manuscript form until it was printed in Ramón, *JFL*, pp. 162-77. In the unpublished article Lalor continued his entreaties to the landlords, while outlining his ideas for an agrarian economy in post-famine Ireland. (NLI, Ms. 340/58).
[97] *Irish Felon*, 1 Jul. 1848. (Ramón, *JFL*, p. 121.)
[98] Ramón, *JFL*, pp. 23-4.
[99] *Irish Felon*, 8 Jul. 1848. (Ramón, *JFL*, p. 132.)

Apart from the human cost which was clear to all, there was also the possible long term damage which the Famine could cause. If starving peasants felt they had nothing to lose by attacking property and stealing food to keep themselves alive, the bonds that held society together would be weakened. As famine spread, religious and legal authorities warned of this danger.[100] For James Fintan Lalor, however, it was already too late. As he wrote in his first article for *The Nation*:

> Society stands dissolved. In effect, as well as of right, it stands dissolved, and another requires to be constituted. To the past we can never return, even if we would.[101]

Although the Famine had led, in Lalor's words, to "social anarchy", he believed that out of it could develop "a thriving and happy community, a solid social economy, a prosperous people, an effective nation".[102] This was the opportunity that Lalor was inviting the landowning class to seize: a new Ireland in which they could participate.

In his unpublished letter of 1844 he had issued a prescient warning to the landlords:

> The sort of necessity which forces men to act whether they will or no, or surrender to it, may not, indeed, have arrived; but any man who is waiting for such a case, requires to be warned that when the final and enforcing necessity for acting comes, it is then commonly too late to act at all, for any good purpose.[103]

By April 1847, "necessity" had indeed arrived and, although Lalor doubted the inclination of the landlords "to act…for any good purpose", he deployed every skill in his literary armoury to cajole, flatter, and shame them into putting the country and its people before their own self-interest. In his first *Nation* article, he repeated the blandishments of his earlier letter. He addressed the landlords as "a national aristocracy", which alone had "the power of framing a new order of arrangement…" As in the 1844 letter, he advised them not to abrogate their

---

[100] See reports in *The Nation*, 1 May 1847: "the sacredness of property must be maintained at all sacrifices, unless we would have society dissolve itself again into its original elements." (Bishop John Hughes of New York), and 8 Jan 1848: "…I do not think it too much to say, that if this state of things [i.e. frauds, intimidation, violence, and murder] were permitted to exist any longer, the bonds of society would be speedily dissolved". (Chief Justice Francis Blackburne).
[101] *Nation*, 24 Apr. 1847. (Ramón, *JFL*, p. 64.)
[102] Ibid. (Ramón, *JFL*, p. 74.)
[103] NLI, Ms. 340/59.

responsibility by passing it on to the English parliament, a body which, he claimed, held them in contempt.[104] While Lalor pressed them to take up their long-neglected position "at the head of this people", he also told the landlords that they were not indispensable in the new Ireland he envisaged, "You are far less important to the people than the people are to you. You cannot stand or act alone, but they can".[105] He described the resentment which their "claims of dominion" engendered among the people, as a result of which they, the landlords, could be "considered specially chargeable with the calamitous crisis that has occurred".[106] If his full meaning was not evident, he invoked the chilling prospect of revolution as had riven France a half-century earlier. Should the landlords refuse to accept the opportunity now being presented to them, "you lie at the feet of events, you lie in the way of a people, and the movement of events and the march of a people shall be over you".[107] As stated above, Lalor toned down his rhetoric on the controversial topics of repeal and land tenure. He equivocated on the former, writing that repeal might deliver "all that Ireland wants" in terms of its prosperity and national pride, or it could lead to "tyranny", but he was not promoting one side or the other. Nevertheless, he implied that he would opt to reject repeal if the question were put to him.[108] On the landholding issue, Lalor made only an oblique reference to his theories in a passage decrying the pre-famine society, where "the earth...with all things therein was made wholly for the few".[109]

Lalor's second *Nation* article presented his own perspective on the Famine and on the role of the landlords in worsening the crisis.[110] Despite his pledge to soften his tone, the new article was more direct than its predecessor and it could hardly have pleased William Smith O'Brien and the other moderates in the Confederation. Lalor accused the landlords of driving their tenants to starvation or emigration by insisting on payment of rent while the potato crop rotted in the ground. He concluded the article with a direct challenge:

> The landowners have adopted the process of depopulating the island, and are pressing it forward to their own destruction, or to ours. They are

---

[104] *Nation*, 24 Apr. 1847. (Ramón, *JFL*, p. 65.)
[105] Ibid. (Ramón, *JFL*, p. 66.)
[106] Ibid.
[107] Ibid. (Ramón, *JFL*, p. 69.)
[108] Ibid. (Ramón, *JFL*, p. 68.) Lalor later accused Duffy of having allowed several misprints into the article, mentioning in particular that "I am made to declare myself an anti-Repealer!" (see Duffy, *Four Years of Irish History*, p. 472.)
[109] *Nation*, 24 Apr. 1847. (Ramón, *JFL*, p. 63.)
[110] *Nation*, 15 May 1847. (Ramón, *JFL*, pp. 78-88.)

declaring that they and we can no longer live together in this land. They are enforcing self-defence on us. They are, at least, forcing on us the question of submission or resistance; and I, for one, shall give my vote for resistance.[111]

Lalor did not follow this uncompromising language through to its logical conclusion by threatening to launch a rent-strike. Instead, he promised to make a "last appeal to the landowners to adopt the only course that can now save a struggle".[112]

Whatever Lalor intended to say to the landlords in his "last appeal" may or may not be contained within his third and final article, which appeared in the 5 June edition of *The Nation*. However, the main impetus behind the piece was an editorial in the same paper, under the headline "A National Council", which Lalor had read following the publication of his second article.[113] The editorial was written by John Mitchel (1815-1875), whom Duffy had hired in October 1845 to replace the recently-deceased Thomas Davis.[114] The editorial dealt with the imminent formation of a Council of National Protection, which was, in effect, a rebranding of a lobby group set up by landlords several months earlier. Its principal demand was that landlords should not have to bear the total cost of the various measures being introduced to alleviate public distress caused by the Famine.[115] Mitchel adopted a similar line to the two articles written by Lalor a few weeks previously. According to Mitchel, the Famine could provide the stimulus for the creation of "order out of this chaos... If landlord and tenant, trader and tradesman, meet in an honest and candid spirit". However, he went further than Lalor by warning of the prospect of "a Jacquerie…involving the universal refusal of rents, and the necessary overturn of society".[116] It seemed that Mitchel was prepared to make explicit a threat that Lalor had hitherto confined to his private correspondence with the Confederation, and only implied in his public utterances. For the moment at least, Lalor kept any exasperation he felt about Mitchel's piece to himself, composing a third article for *The Nation* which stuck to the relatively measured tone of its predecessors. In it, Lalor acknowledged the potential of the new landlord body, but only if it formed part of a national assembly that also included representatives of tenant farmers and tradesmen.[117] Of course, Lalor was interested primarily in the

---

[111] Ibid. (Ramón, *JFL*, p. 88.)
[112] Ibid.
[113] *Nation*, 22 May 1847.
[114] Quinn, *Young Ireland*, p. 89.
[115] O'Neill, *JFL*, pp. 62-3.
[116] *Nation*, 22 May 1847.
[117] O'Neill, *JFL*, p. 65. Ramón, *JFL*, p. 21.

former and he set out how they might organise themselves to form one half of what he termed "the Commons of Ireland". The first step, according to Lalor, would be the creation of tenant leagues in each county. From these would be appointed a national committee authorised to negotiate with the landlords on behalf of the tenant farmers. Lalor recognised that his proposal was probably illegal under the terms of the Convention Act of 1793, which forbade any assemblies that might compete with the British Parliament. However, he concluded his short article with an expression of hope that his suggestions could be carried out in such a way as to avoid breaking the law.[118]

As is clear from this brief examination, Lalor adhered more or less to his agreement with Duffy that his articles for *The Nation* would not conflict with Confederation policy regarding the landlords. He also held back from expressing the full force of his radical ideas on land and independence. However, the Confederation was well aware of Lalor's views on these matters from his private letters to them. Four of the surviving letters, addressed to Duffy, McGee and Mitchel, anticipated the content of Lalor's *Irish Felon* articles, published over a year later. An analysis of these letters bears out Duffy's judgement as to their extreme content.

Lalor's "private exhortations and remonstrances"

Lalor regarded with disdain both O'Connell's Repeal Association and the repeal objective itself. In his first letter to Gavan Duffy, he described O'Connell as a "traitor" and characterised him and his associates as "intrinsically and essentially vile and base". What is more, he went on, "I will never contribute one shilling, or give my name, heart, or hand, for such an object as the simple Repeal by the British Parliament of the Act of Union". Lalor tried to persuade Duffy and his colleagues that it was pointless to pursue the same objective as O'Connell's association. First of all, neither group had a clear strategy to induce Britain to concede repeal. Secondly, the majority of the people, suffering under Famine as they were, could not care less about repeal and no one would take up arms to fight for it.[119] Even if it were achievable, repeal held no attractions for Lalor, as he made clear in those early private letters to the Confederation leaders: "Two independent co-equal, and sovereign legislatures, forming one state under one crown, is an arrangement repugnant alike to common sense

---

[118] *Nation*, 5 Jun. 1847. (Ramón, *JFL*, pp. 89-92.)
[119] JFL to Duffy, 11 Jan. 1847, RIA 12.P.15/6.

and experience".[120] What he wanted instead he described in another letter to John Mitchel dated 21 June 1847:

> My object is to repeal the Conquest—not any particular part or portion but the whole and entire conquest of seven hundred years—a thing much more easily done than to repeal the Union.[121]

He did not, however, advocate permanent separation from Britain. He proposed a federal union between the two countries, to be negotiated only after Ireland had achieved independence.

In his second letter to Duffy and his colleagues, Lalor outlined this somewhat surprising idea: "…full and entire independence, is a necessary preliminary to any permanent, or satisfactory arrangement with Britain. The steps are—independence, negotiation, and federal union."[122] Several years earlier the Repeal Association had been embroiled in an internal dispute over the question of a future federal arrangement between Ireland and Britain. In 1844 O'Connell briefly advocated federalism in deference to unionist concerns about the more radical form of separation implicit in the repeal objective. However, Duffy criticised the proposal publicly in the pages of *The Nation* and O'Connell dropped it.[123] Why then did Lalor revive an idea that even moderates like Duffy rejected as having been "calculated to perpetuate our moral and intellectual subjection to England"?[124] Lalor's precedent was the relationship between American states such as New York and Pennsylvania entered into under the terms of the then-US Constitution. It may have seemed to Lalor that membership of a federation of states along the lines of the US model would not dilute national sovereignty.[125] However, in 1918, Arthur Griffith criticised Lalor's proposal, pointing out that "New York and Pennsylvania have a Washington above them".[126] Nevertheless Lalor made it clear in his letter that

---

[120] *Irish Felon*, 1 Jul. 1848. (Ramón, *JFL*, p. 122.).
[121] JFL to Mitchel, 21 Jun. 1847, RIA 12.P.15/7.
[122] *Irish Felon*, 1 Jul. 1848 (Ramón, *JFL*, p. 123).
[123] Kinealy, *Repeal and Revolution*, pp. 40-1.
[124] Charles Gavan Duffy, *Young Ireland: a Fragment of Irish history, 1840-1850* (London, 1880), p. 581.
[125] Lalor's understanding of the US Constitution may have been drawn from his reading of Cyrus R. Edmonds, *The Life and Times of General Washington* (2 vols, London, 1835-6), a copy of which was included in a catalogue of books held in Tinakill and compiled in 1860.
[126] Fogarty, *JFL*, p. vii. Griffith did not consider the extent to which state power was subsequently made subservient to the federal government by the 14th Amendment of 1868. (See Randall G. Holcombe, *From Liberty to Democracy: the Transformation of American Government* (Ann Arbor, MI., 2002), pp. 122-4).

any federal union would be negotiated by two independent and equal states, and would not be subject to terms set by an "Imperial (British) Parliament".[127] His proposal may have been made in order to appease a nationalist leadership who were content to see Ireland remain subject to the British Crown. As Duffy noted later, even Mitchel in 1847 was not contemplating complete separation, let alone a republic.[128] Whatever his reasoning may have been, there is no record of Lalor ever repeating his proposal. More to the point, however, is that he was not only urging the Irish Confederation to adopt his policy of full independence, he was also offering a previously unheard of strategy to achieve it, that is, the land question.

It is not known when Lalor first formulated his famous principle about the land of Ireland belonging to the people of Ireland. But the first extant expression of it is in a letter dated 13 March 1847 addressed to Thomas D'Arcy McGee (1825-1868).

> My principle is this, that the entire ownership of Ireland, moral and material, up to the sun and down to the centre, is vested by right in the people of Ireland—that they and none but they are landowners and lawmakers of this island; that all laws not made by them are null and void, and all titles to land are invalid not conferred or confirmed by them; and that the full right of owners may and must be asserted and enforced by any and all means which God has put in the power of man.[129]

Lalor realised that, to a moderate repealer such as McGee, his principle would seem subversive: "Your reason may assent, yet your feelings revolt". However, he also pointed out that any landlord could retain his holdings if he swore allegiance to the Irish people. In his letter to Mitchel of 21 June, Lalor spelt out his principle in even more direct terms:

> … the absolute (allodial) ownership of the lands of Ireland is vested of right in the people of Ireland — that they, and none but they, are the first landowners and lords paramount as well as the lawmakers of this island.[130]

Lalor's use of the terms "allodial" and "lords paramount" underlined that, for him, the Irish people, and not the British monarch, were the ultimate authority in respect of landholding. "As a republican", wrote O'Neill, "he eliminated the

---

[127] *Irish Felon*, 1 Jul. 1848. (Ramón, *JFL*, p. 123).
[128] Duffy, *Four Years of Irish History*, p. 170.
[129] JFL to McGee, 13 Mar. 1847, NLI, Ms. 340/61.
[130] JFL to Mitchel, 21 Jun. 1847, RIA 12.P.15/7.

king and modified feudal law accordingly".[131] However, a more urgent issue needed to be addressed if Lalor's principles were ever to be implemented. In the same letter, he reminded Mitchel that only two months remained before the likely return of the blight, and the wiping out of the putative army of tenant farmers on whom they depended. That time would be needed to organise the farmers whereas, it seemed to Lalor from the previous month's *Nation* editorial, Mitchel was banking on "an unprepared, disorderly and vile jacquerie" to take on the landlords, should they resist. Already, according to Lalor, "the bailiff follows in the track of the reaper". He complained that Mitchel and his colleagues were offering no help in forming the tenant leagues which he, Lalor, had proposed in the third of his *Nation* letters as a necessary counterweight to the landlord's council.[132]

Setback at Holy Cross

By August, Lalor's continuous badgering of the Confederation produced some results as he reported to his brother, Richard: "After a long correspondence with Mitchel and Devin Reilly, they have at length agreed to aid and support me, in a mode concerted between us".[133] On 8 September, a Tipperary newspaper carried a notice from "Mr. Lalor, son of Mr. Lalor of Tenakill" (sic) which stated "that a County Meeting is to be held at Holy Cross on Sunday the 19th of September to form a County Tenant League".[134] It was widely expected that Lalor would use the meeting to publicly call for a rent strike. Tenant farmers in the county were reported to be already withholding rent payments in anticipation of such a move.[135] The evidence suggests that the rumours and reports were correct. In a 16-page draft speech, which Lalor presumably intended to deliver at the Tipperary meeting, he employed his considerable rhetorical gifts in support of a number of far-reaching principles and propositions, as this extract illustrates:

> Will gallant Tipperary yield up house and home and land and life without even a struggle at the bidding of strangers? Will her people surrender and sink into paupers? Will they deliver up the land they have spent their lives on. Will they deliver up the harvest they have spent their labour on. Will they deliver up the whole of it at a word or command in

---

[131] O'Neill, "Irish Land Question", pp. 332-3.
[132] JFL to Mitchel, 21 Jun. 1847, RIA 12.P.15/7.
[133] JFL to RL, 21 Aug. 1847, NLI, Ms. 8563/2.
[134] *Tipperary Vindicator*, 8 Sep. 1847.
[135] Ramón, *JFL*, p. 24.

the shape of rents and rates? I say no. I say no for myself, I say no for you, I say no for Tipperary, I say no for Ireland.[136]

Underlining the seriousness of the perceived threat, *The Times* of London devoted its lead editorial to a denunciation of Lalor, "a clever and eloquent incendiary", whose aim seemed to the leader-writer to be the "ousting of landlords or abolition of rent".[137] On the eve of the meeting, the new chairman of the Repeal Association, John O'Connell, implored tenants to reject "the instigation of incendiaries amongst yourselves, urging you to refuse the payment of rents".[138] If anyone doubted his authority to make such a call, O'Connell invoked the memory of his recently-deceased father, Daniel, in what O'Neill described as "almost an *ex-cathedra* statement".[139]

Whether or not these interventions were a factor, the turnout for Lalor's rally was disappointing. In a letter written shortly beforehand, Lalor had confidently predicted an "enormous" gathering of at least 10,000 supporters.[140] According to one newspaper, press reporters who attended expressed surprise "at the comparative paucity of the number assembled", which was estimated at about 4,000 tenant farmers.[141] Despite the extensive preparations evident in his surviving notes, Lalor spoke only briefly and made no mention of a rent strike. Instead, the proceedings were dominated by Michael Doheny (1805-1862), a member of the Irish Confederation council who was also a Tipperary farmer and lawyer. Doheny had collaborated closely with Lalor during the weeks leading up to the meeting.[142] Nevertheless the surviving correspondence between the two men indicates considerable disagreement as to what strategies and tactics the proposed tenant league should put into effect. In one letter, Doheny set the limit of his cooperation at the "adoption of the tenant right", which of course was the mainstay of Confederation policy on the land question. He was not prepared to advocate a refusal to pay rent in support of this objective.[143] It seems that Lalor was persuaded by Doheny's implied threat to withdraw and, as Ramón concluded, agreed to soften his approach.[144] Doheny himself set the tone by

---

[136] NLI, Ms. 340/48
[137] *The Times*, 14 Sep. 1847.
[138] *Freeman's Journal*, 18 Sep. 1847.
[139] O'Neill, *JFL*, p. 73.
[140] *Tipperary Vindicator*, 30 Apr. 1867.
[141] Ibid., 22 Sep. 1847.
[142] Ramón, *JFL*, p. 24.
[143] Doheny to JFL, NLI, Ms. 340/27.
[144] Ramón, *JFL*, p. 26.

declaring at the start of his lengthy remarks that the meeting would not mark "the beginning of a crusade against rents".[145]

Notwithstanding these setbacks, Lalor managed to achieve some success in the framing of the 11 resolutions adopted by the assembly, most of which he proposed.[146] They are an incongruous mix of Confederation aims, such as tenant right, and Lalor's own more idealistic principles.[147] Collectively they illustrate the tensions that existed between Lalor and his Confederation associates and, perhaps also, within Lalor's own mind. Resolutions one and six reflected the theories of landholding which Lalor had hitherto articulated only in private in his letters to D'Arcy McGee and Mitchel. Although couched in more guarded and legalistic language than his previous formulations, these two resolutions marked Lalor's determination to establish his principles in the public record. Thus, the first resolution declared that "the soil of Ireland belongs to the people of Ireland" while, in the sixth, Lalor defined the limits on "any right of private property in the substance of the soil" to whatever laws might be enacted by the will of the people. Apart from these statements of principle, Lalor achieved one other modest success, but it was a pyrrhic victory. Following Doheny's proposal of the seventh resolution, which called for the extension to Tipperary of the terms of the Ulster Custom, Lalor added a proviso apparently intended to prevent landlords imposing excessive rents. However, the wording is so clumsy and imprecise as to suggest a hastily-drafted compromise over the rent issue between the two organisers. The result was the eighth resolution in which Lalor proposed that a "fairly constituted and impartial tribunal" would fix the amount of rent to be paid. However, without the leverage of a rent strike to extract such a concession, or an acceptable state authority to enforce it, the only option left to Lalor was to leave it to an "agreement between landlord and tenant" to determine how such an arbitration system would operate in practice.[148] To further underline the extent to which he had diluted his principles, the ninth resolution left it up to the landlords themselves as to whether or not they would support the introduction of tenant right into the county.[149] These motions, although proposed by Lalor, were entirely consistent with Doheny's evident desire to retain the goodwill of the landlords. As he stated in his address,

---

[145] *Freeman's Journal*, 20 Sep. 1847.
[146] Ibid.
[147] *Tipperary Vindicator*, 22 Sep. 1847.
[148] *Freeman's Journal*, 20 Sep. 1847.
[149] Ibid.

> I say boldly that I look upon the landlords as a class of my own countrymen, and that I would not sacrifice any class (cheers). I seek to do them no injustice, but the contrary.[150]

Following the Holy Cross meeting, much commentary appeared in the national and provincial press, some hopeful about the prospects for tenant farmers[151], others condemnatory of Lalor's "revolutionary" aims.[152] As for the poor turnout, a local newspaper argued that "[the people of Tipperary] will shun the man against whom their clergy caution them".[153] Indeed, the various reports of the meeting do not refer to any priest or minister among those on the platform.[154] However, the most pointed verdict appeared in another editorial which *The Times* devoted to Lalor and his "utterly impractical courses". According to the writer, the proceedings were "vague, gusty, pointless, and intemperate".[155] Harsh as it may have seemed, the London newspaper's conclusion was an apt judgment on an agenda that was clearly an attempt at a compromise between two irreconcilable viewpoints. The contradiction was clear to James MacGrady, a friend of the Lalor family, who in a letter to a local paper wrote, "I do not think that the demand for the Tenant Right of Ulster came up, or nearly up to the abstract propositions advanced in the opening resolutions".[156] If Lalor had unveiled for the first time in a public setting his vision of a new system of landholding in Ireland, he could not explain how the beleaguered tenant farmers could collectively realise that vision. His bitterness at the lack of support from the nationalist leaders he had courted for months is evident in his final letter to Doheny:

> Tell your friends of the Confederation that they have surrendered up their country without a blow. I wish them all a good night and gay dreams.[157]

In Ramón's words, Lalor "admitted defeat and returned to Tinnakill".[158]

Lalor and *The Irish Felon*

In her invaluable survey of the Dublin newspaper industry during the nineteenth century, Ann Andrews wrote that "James Fintan Lalor… was

---

[150] Ibid.
[151] Ibid.
[152] *Tipperary Vindicator*, 22 Sep. 1847.
[153] Ibid.
[154] *Freeman's Journal*, 20 Sep. 1847. *Nenagh Guardian*, 22 Sep. 1847.
[155] *The Times*, 22 Sep. 1847.
[156] *Tipperary Vindicator*, 6 Oct. 1847.
[157] JFL to Doheny, 10 Nov. 1847, NAI OP/1848/105/6.
[158] Ramón, *JFL*, p. 28.

possessed of an almost obsessive belief that a newspaper was essential to disseminate his views…"[159] This was not an uncommon conviction among European nationalists at this time. In Italy, Giuseppe Mazzini, a leading political activist and thinker, was equally preoccupied with the unique power of the press to "move… the human soul". Mazzini was deeply involved in the printing of newspapers and pamphlets throughout his long campaign to bring public opinion behind his goal of a free and united Italy.[160] Although pamphleteering was also a popular means of disseminating ideas and opinions in early nineteenth-century Ireland, Lalor was apparently not interested in that alternative channel. Perhaps the contemporary perception of the pamphlet as a conduit for moral and religious instruction was off-putting to someone bent on the transformation of society.[161] On the other hand, Lalor's "experiment" to harness the power and reach of *The Nation* had clearly failed. The chief factor in that failure was his dependence on "gatekeepers', such as Duffy and Doheny, who would not support the radical ideas he wished to propagate.[162] However, in the early summer of 1848, an opportunity arose that would allow Lalor to wield greater control over the circulation of his ideas. It was enough to entice him out of his Tinakill redoubt and back into the public realm.

In its edition of 17 June, *The Nation* carried on its front page an advertisement for a new weekly journal to be known as *The Irish Felon*. According to the notice, the new organ would be "edited by John Martin, aided by Thomas Devin Reilly, James F. Lalor".[163] Martin and Reilly stood at the more radical end of contemporary Irish nationalism. Along with John Mitchel, they left the Confederation early in 1848 and set up their own newspaper, *The United Irishman*, in opposition to *The Nation*. Although the new periodical achieved a large circulation, its support for violent revolution provoked swift action by the authorities and it was closed down after 16 editions.[164] Notwithstanding its radical editorial policy, *The United Irishman's* line on landholding was close to

---

[159] Andrews, *Newspapers and Newsmakers*, p. 135.
[160] Lucy Riall, *Garibaldi: Invention of a Hero* (New Haven, Conn., 2007), pp. 29-30.
[161] Charles Benson and Siobhán Fitzpatrick, "Pamphlets", in James H. Murphy (ed.), *The Oxford History of the Irish Book: volume 4: the Irish book in English, 1800-1891* (Oxford, 2011), pp. 139-143.
[162] Duffy ensured that Lalor's name was appended to his articles in *The Nation* because, as Duffy wrote later, he "did not agree with them". Unsigned articles, such as leading articles, were assumed to reflect the opinions of the editor who would then be morally responsible for their content. (see Charles Gavan Duffy, *My Life in Two Hemispheres* (2 vols., New York, 1898), i, p. 242.)
[163] *Nation*, 17 Jun. 1848.
[164] Andrews, *Newspapers and Newsmakers*, pp. 115-22.

that of the Confederation and *The Nation*. The paper promoted the expansion of tenant right from its Ulster base to the rest of the country, but rejected the widely-held belief that the practice was of British origin. Instead, the paper argued, tenant right "was the ancient custom of Ireland since before Saint Patrick". It had survived in Ulster, the paper alleged, because that province was the last to be conquered.[165] When *The United Irishman* was suppressed in late-May, Mitchel was arrested, prosecuted, and sent into exile for 14 years.[166] Martin and Reilly invited Lalor to join them in setting up another paper that would continue in *The United Irishman*'s footsteps. The founders of *The Irish Felon* capitalised on the wave of public support for Mitchel that followed his transportation by adding the legend "Successor to *The United Irishman*" to its masthead. The strategy worked and sales of the new paper exceeded those of its predecessor.[167]

Although Lalor's new associates were more sympathetic to his ideas, some compromise on his part was still necessary, at least at first. The advertisement for *The Irish Felon* included 12 principles which the founders undertook to follow.[168] Perhaps inevitably, the fifth of these involved the promotion of tenant right across the country. However it was preceded by four reiterations of Lalor's theories on landholding, the first offering a variation on his familiar doctrine, i.e. "that the Irish people have a just and indefeasible right to this island, and to all the moral and material wealth and resources thereof…" The sixth principle may also reflect Lalor's influence in that it seems to anticipate his subsequent radical proposals on the payment of rent. It stated "that every man in Ireland who shall hereafter pay taxes for the support of the State, shall have a just right to an equal voice with every other man in the government of that State, and the outlay of those taxes". In one of his first letters to the Confederation Lalor had bemoaned the absence of any "direct and general state-tax, payment of which might be refused and resisted".[169] If self-rule were achieved, however, the wording of the sixth principle indicates that Lalor viewed the payment of tax as

---

[165] *United Irishman*, 1 Apr. 1848.
[166] James Quinn, "Mitchel, John", *DIB* (Cambridge, 2012), (http://dib.cambridge.org/viewReadPage.do?articleId=a5834) 6 Jun. 2017.
[167] Andrews, *Newspapers and Newsmakers*, p. 126.
[168] *Nation*, 17 Jun. 1848.
[169] *Irish Felon*, 1 Jul. 1848. (Ramón, *JFL*, p. 121). Ireland had been exempted from the Income Tax Act 1842 which imposed a levy of 7% on incomes of £150 per annum. (see B. E. V. Sabine, *History of Income Tax: the Development of Income Tax from its Beginning in 1799 to the Present Day related to the Social, Economic and Political History of the Period* (Oxford, 2006), pp. 60-2.)

conferring rights on citizens, rural and urban, thus giving them a stake in the governance of their country.

Notwithstanding his input into the 12 principles underpinning the new paper, Lalor also felt it necessary to set out his own manifesto because, as he put it, "It is requisite the paper should have but one object and that the public should understand what that object is". Lalor submitted his terms to the editor John Martin in the form of a letter and it was published in the first edition of *The Irish Felon*.[170] In it, he outlined "the principles and conditions, public and personal on which alone I would desire to be accepted as a partner in this undertaking". For the first time in print, Lalor defined his thinking on repeal and land tenure in language that up to now he had confined to his private correspondence with the Confederation. The letter is remarkable as much for what it leaves out as for what it includes. Whereas a year earlier he had dissembled on the question of repeal in his first article for *The Nation*, now he wrote in terms redolent of his early letters to the Confederation. Repeal was "utterly impracticable" because "the country-peasantry will never arm and fight for it—neither will I". Lalor reiterated the greater objective he had revealed in his letter to Mitchel 12 months previously, i.e. "Not to repeal the Union, then, but to repeal the Conquest". As Ramón has argued, Lalor did not see the English conquest as solely representing political hegemony over the Irish people, but as the appropriation of the land itself by an elite class who owed their loyalty to the British crown.[171] Consequently, Lalor once again emphasised the link between national sovereignty and the land question: "My wish is to combine and cement the two into one; and so, perfect, and reinforce, and carry both". For Lalor this meant restoring the land to the "nation at large". There was no point in continuing to appease the current landlords who, he asserted, demanded their rents even if their tenants starved as a result. In his most uncompromising language to date, Lalor characterised them as "Strangers…in this land they call theirs". If they switched allegiance to the Irish people, they might retain their property "in fee from the Irish nation". Otherwise, they must leave Ireland; whether they would be compensated or not Lalor left unsaid. For Lalor, the national crisis made such a binary decision inescapable—"They or we must quit this island". However, he also realised that his new partners, not to mention his readership, might baulk at such a stark ultimatum. Perhaps in order to avoid alienating his audience, he tempered his closing remarks on the subject of land tenure so as to leave open the question of whether or not he supported the commonly-held principle of private property in land.

---

[170] *Irish Felon*, 24 Jun. 1848 (Ramón, *JFL*, pp. 96-108.)
[171] Ramón, *JFL*, p. 23.

Nonetheless, what he had to say on the topic in his open letter to *The Irish Felon* was more radical than anything he had yet allowed into the public domain.

Having restated the principle that "the entire soil of a country belongs of right to the people of that country", Lalor addressed the issue of property rights. Firstly, he maintained that "No one has more respect for the real rights of property than I have". However, such "real rights" did not extend to what he called the "robber's right" of occupation under which "eight thousand persons" could "abrogate the rights of a numerous people…[i.e.] a population of eight millions". His use of the term "in fee" to describe the basis on which anyone might hold land under the new regime he was putting forward could imply that he was proposing nothing more than freehold or unconditional ownership, albeit by a greater number of tenant farmers. Similarly, the omission of any mention of tenant right would not necessarily have suggested to his readers that he no longer supported the policy. However, in light of his subsequent writings on landholding and land tenure, these points could also be interpreted as deliberate obfuscation on Lalor's part. He was alive to the danger of losing support if his ideas went beyond what his readership was prepared to accept at that time. As he wrote in his next piece in *The Irish Felon*:

> The very foremost banner should never be too far forward. In advance, but not miles nor months in advance — a stride before his regiment, a day before his people — this is a leader's place.[172]

Publication of his letter seemed to increase Lalor's confidence and he followed it with another six letters and articles, each more radical than the last. Of these, three dealt with the land question. One has already been discussed above as it was circulated privately among Irish Confederation leaders in January 1847.[173] Of the other two, the first comprised a brief restatement of the principles of landholding laid out in the previous week's edition of *The Irish Felon*. The main thrust of the piece, however, was a call to readers to form armed militias across the country in case of an attack by Crown forces.[174] The remaining article is perhaps Lalor's most famous. It appeared in the edition of 8 July under the headline, "The Faith of a Felon". It was to be his last word, at least in public, on the land question.

---

[172] *Irish Felon*, 1 Jul. 1848 (Ramón, *JFL*, p. 110.)
[173] Ibid., (Ramón, *JFL*, pp. 113-26.)
[174] Ibid., (Ramón, *JFL*, pp. 109-12.)

"The Faith of a Felon"

Just as Charles Gavan Duffy was instrumental in bringing James Fintan Lalor into print for the first time, so he was also the catalyst for the writing of "The Faith of a Felon". In its edition of 29 April 1848, *The Nation* published an article by Duffy under the headline, "The Creed of 'The Nation'". [175] As the title suggests, Duffy wanted to set out the guiding principles behind the newspaper in order to refute charges by the British government that its nationalist policy would lead to a type of Jacobin anarchy. Nevertheless, Duffy foresaw revolution as "inevitable… either by negotiation or the sword". But it would be a revolution with repeal, not total separation, as its objective: "a sovereign state… under the sway of the Crown". Even if a military uprising were necessary, Duffy sought to reassure what he referred to as "the capitalist, the merchant, [and] the trader" that he and his colleagues had no desire to create a new society in which their private property would be plundered. On the contrary, he maintained that "the rights of private property, the just rights of every class in the state will be sacred". As for landowners, they should embrace repeal and benefit from the increased productivity that would follow the establishment by an Irish parliament of tenant right. So while Duffy was explicitly allowing for the use of force to achieve the aims of the Irish Confederation, the outcome—if revolution were actually necessary—would not disturb unduly the current order of society. Now that he had access to a national newspaper, Lalor decided to answer Duffy's "Creed" with a statement of his own quite different beliefs.[176]

In the introduction to his article, Lalor wrote that he would have preferred more time to shape and polish the piece. However, fearing imminent arrest, he "hasten[ed] to put my own principles upon record". What appeared in *The Irish Felon* of 8 July was intended to be the first of a two-part article, the second to be published in the following week's edition. However on the very day that the first part appeared, the police raided *The Irish Felon* office in Trinity Street, Dublin, and the remainder of Lalor's article was seized. Even though it is unfinished, "The Faith of a Felon" contains the most complete and unbridled exposition of Lalor's thinking. It has been reproduced, in part or in whole, many times since first publication, mostly by admirers and scholars. But the first extract appeared in *The Times* of London in its report of the police raid. The paper's stance is clear from its description of Lalor as "the most felonious of the [*Irish Felon's*] contributors", and as an "indefatigable treason-monger".[177]

---

[175] *Nation*, 29 Apr. 1848.
[176] *Irish Felon*, 8 Jul. 1848 (Ramón, *JFL*, pp. 131-42.)
[177] *The Times*, 10 Jul. 1848.

In "The Faith of a Felon", Lalor agreed with Duffy's acceptance of armed rebellion, but rejected the latter's political objectives.

> ...by force of arms alone can [independence] ever be achieved; and never on the Repeal question will you see men stand in array of battle against England.[178]

Lalor dismissed Mitchel's depiction, in *The United Irishman*, of the Ulster Custom as an indigenous practice that preceded English jurisdiction. While he conceded that it conferred some advantage on tenants in that province, he also insisted that those tenants were colonisers and "the settlement that prevails was made by a sort of consent and agreement among the conquering race".[179] He reaffirmed the principle of landholding which he had first set down in his letter to D'Arcy McGee a year-and-a-half earlier, and restated several times since. But he went further even than his first *Irish Felon* letter by defining what he meant by the right of private property. That right, he contended, referred to what a man "has himself CREATED". If this seems like a restatement of the terms of the Ulster Custom, under which a tenant-owned any improvements he made to his landlord's property, Lalor showed in his next sentence how far beyond such a measure his thinking went. "This title", he wrote, "is the *sole* and *only* title by which a valid right of absolute private property can possibly vest." In other words, as no man could create land, so he could never own it. Lalor expanded on this point as follows:

> The earth together with all it spontaneously produces is the free and common property of all mankind, of natural right, and by the grant of God; and, all men being equal, no man, therefore, has a right to appropriate exclusively to himself any part or portion thereof, except with the common consent and agreement of all other men.[180]

This "common consent and agreement" were necessary because the people were, as Lalor had already stated in his letter to Mitchel, "first proprietors and lords paramount". But even they could not grant ownership irrevocably and in perpetuity to any individual, because as he wrote, "no generation of living men can bind a generation that is yet unborn, or can sell or squander the rights of man; and each generation of men has but a life interest in the world". For Lalor, the way to realise his vision might begin with a rent-strike by tenant-farmers, but it would not end there. Lalor wrote that, in a self-governing, fully independent nation, the people should decide "in national congress or convention... what rents they are

---

[178] *Irish Felon*, 8 Jul. 1848 (Ramón, *JFL*, pp. 136-7.)
[179] Ibid. (Ramón, *JFL*, p. 141.)
[180] Ibid. (Ramón, *JFL*, pp. 137-8.)

to pay, and to whom they are to pay them". He then made his own position clear in the following statement:

> And that the people on grounds of policy and economy, ought to decide (as a general rule, admitting of reservations) that those rents shall be paid to themselves, the people, for public purposes, and for behoof and benefit of them, the entire general people.[181]

While he acknowledged that such a demand might not be warranted by the immediate crisis, he was also unapologetic about articulating what some of his readers might regard as an irrelevant aspiration. In fact, Lalor was looking beyond the here and now, terrible as it was. "I view it as ages will view it not through the mists of famine but by the living lights of the firmament." He then predicted that if Ireland took the path he was suggesting, the impact on the world would equal that of the French Revolution.

> Mankind will yet be masters of the earth. The right of the people to make the laws—this produced the first great modern earthquake, whose latest shocks even now are heaving the heart of the world. The right of the people to own the land—this will produce the next.[182]

Notwithstanding the incomplete and hurried nature of the article, in one significant passage, it acted as a bookend to his first letter to Gavan Duffy a year-and-a-half earlier. In that letter, Lalor predicted that, if his ideas on the land question were embraced, Ireland would become

> an original inventor, propounder, and propagandist, in the van of the earth, and heading the nations; on which her success or her failure alike would never be forgotten by man, but would make her, for ever, the lode star of history.[183]

Now that he had finally unveiled those ideas in full, Lalor repeated almost verbatim the same vision for Ireland.

> I want to put Ireland foremost, in the van of the world, at the head of the nations, to set her aloft in the blaze of the sun, and to make her for ages the lode star of history.[184]

The similarity between these two passages demonstrates how confident Lalor was from the start that, if they were accepted in his native country, his radical ideas about land tenure and property rights would have a profound impact

---

[181] Ibid. (Ramón, *JFL*, p. 134.)
[182] Ibid. (Ramón, *JFL*, p. 135.)
[183] JFL to Duffy, 11 Jan. 1847, RIA 12.P.15/6.
[184] *Irish Felon*, 8 Jul. 1848 (Ramón, *JFL*, p. 135.)

beyond Ireland's shores. Prompted by Gavan Duffy's frank "Creed", Lalor cast aside the ambiguity that has caused so much confusion to later interpreters of his work and revealed himself to be, in all but name, both a republican and an advocate of land nationalisation.

Lalor the revolutionary

While this was his last word in print on the subject of land reform, the land question continued to prey on Lalor's mind during the remainder of his short life. However, his final two published pieces, which appeared in *The Irish Felon* on 15 and 22 July respectively, were concerned with revolution. Nationalist sentiment had intensified over the summer of 1848, drawing even moderates like William Smith O'Brien into preparations for "armed resistance to the oppressors of our country".[185] This hardening of anti-British feeling followed Mitchel's arrest and deportation in May. Of course, the revolutionary fervour that spread across Europe during, what *The Economist* magazine referred to as, "the most eventful year in the history of modern Europe" contributed also to the growing anticipation of imminent insurrection.[186] On 15 July, *The Nation* reported the arrests of several Confederation leaders, including Charles Gavan Duffy.[187] On 20 July, martial law was declared in Dublin, and within days encompassed other major cities. Lalor himself was arrested on 28 July and eventually incarcerated in Dublin's Newgate Prison where he was held until his release on health grounds four months later.[188]

For much of 1849 Lalor devoted his energies to the cause of revolution. This entailed travelling through the country in a bid to recruit new blood for another insurrection; the Young Ireland rising at Ballingarry on 29 July 1848 had been an ignominious failure. Among his "comrades-in-arms" during this process were two young nationalists who would go on to become leading figures in the Irish republican movement: John O'Leary and Thomas Clarke Luby. Both wrote later of their conversations with Lalor, including those on the land question. O'Leary was less interested in this topic than his older associate, as this passage from his memoirs attests:

---

[185] William Smith O'Brien, "Address of the Council of the Irish Confederation to the Irish People", reprinted in John Savage, *'98 and '48: the Modern Revolutionary History and Literature of Ireland. Third edition, with an appendix and index* (New York, 1856), Appendix XI, p. 404.
[186] Quoted in Kinealy, *Repeal and Revolution*, p. 2.
[187] *Nation*, 15 Jul. 1848.
[188] O'Neill, *JFL*, pp. 87-96.

much of [our talk] was political, and some of it politico-economical, owing to Lalor's peculiar theories on the land question ... and when I began to discuss Lalor's theories with himself, I found my agrarian ardour fast cooling down, and finally disappearing altogether.[189]

The more sympathetic Luby recalled his time with Lalor in a series of newspaper articles published more than 30 years after the events they described. Luby went further than O'Leary with his memory of a specific conversation that illustrates Lalor's continuing preoccupation with the land question:

'In strict ethics,' said Lalor, 'the Irish peasantry would, no doubt, be entitled to demand for themselves a total resumption of the ownership of the soil of Ireland. But, to prevent harrassing strife and trouble and bad blood, not to speak of risk and expense, it would be undoubtedly wise to compromise with the landlords, if only these last would even now have the sense to meet us half way.'[190]

Despite the quotation marks, Luby entered the caveat that "This is the substance, if not the exact words, of what he said". Nevertheless, Luby appreciated Lalor's philosophy of landholding better than most of his contemporaries. In an 1855 newspaper article, Luby restated Lalor's principle that the land cannot become the property of any individual and must belong to "the Nation [which] may, when it likes, resume every acre of it for the purpose of a re-distribution".[191] So he well understood that what Lalor was advocating was much more radical than tenant right or even peasant proprietorship. Therefore, Luby's retelling of Lalor's comment is probably a true reflection of his friend's thinking at a time when he was wrestling still with the issues he had written about a year before.

Even as he planned violent insurrection it seems, according to Luby's report, that Lalor hankered after compromise and peace. Despite his dogmatic assertions about land tenure and property rights, he would have settled for something less than his ideal solution, if it meant sparing the country the turmoil that armed revolution would bring with it. But if Lalor did sometimes entertain thoughts about what might be, he also recognised the harsh reality around him. He saw an obdurate landowning class, backed by an increasingly overbearing British state, blocking the Irish people from control over the very soil on which they depended for life itself. That necessitated new thinking, indeed a new Ireland in which the old ways no longer applied. In linking land

---

[189] John O'Leary, *Recollections of Fenians and Fenianism*, (2 vols., London, 1896), i, pp. 37-8.
[190] *Irish Nation*, 28 Jan. 1882.
[191] *Tribune*, 17 Nov. 1855 (quoted in Ramón, *JFL*, p. 47.)

reform and independence as twin objectives, Lalor realised that the former could not be achieved without the latter. If the people were to be "first proprietors and lords paramount", British hegemony had to be ended. It was logical, therefore, that he should devote the remainder of his life, not to the organisation of farmers' rallies in pursuit of security of tenure, but to the primary goal of achieving national sovereignty. Only after full independence could the people dispose of the land as they saw fit, but that prize would not be easily won. In his final published article, which he entitled "Clearing Decks", Lalor dismissed those who warned against "premature, imprudent, or dangerous… act[s] of resistance". There could never be, Lalor insisted, a right time for insurrection, but "*somewhere*, and *somehow*, and by *somebody*, a *beginning must be* made…"[192]

"This island-Queen"

In both his private communications with Young Ireland and his published articles in the press, Lalor advanced a novel concept of nationality and nationhood that has been overlooked by his contemporaries and by later commentators.[193] This was his repeated use of what may be termed the "queen-metaphor". The earliest surviving example can be found in his letter to McGee of 13 March 1847. In driving home to McGee his point that landed property should become subject to the will of the Irish people, Lalor used a striking image:

> I would make Ireland, in fact, as she is in right, mistress and queen of all those lands—that she is a lady of soft heart and grateful disposition and may, in reward of allegiance, confer new titles or confirm the old.[194]

Two months later he again employed the queen-metaphor in his letter to John Mitchel, adding the warning that those landlords who refused "to swear allegiance to this island-Queen… should cease to be landowners or quit this land".[195] Lalor did not confine references to the "queen" to his private correspondence with the Confederation. In his first article for *The Nation* he reminded landowners that Ireland was their "own mother-country". In his attempt to persuade them to rethink their traditional loyalties, Lalor urged the landlords to regard the "Queen-island" as their rightful sovereign. As stated previously, at first Lalor adhered to the Confederation policy of trying to win landlord support and so, in the same article, he flatteringly portrayed them as

---

[192] *Irish Felon*, 22 Jul. 1848 (Ramón, *JFL*, pp. 148-52.)
[193] Only O'Neill and Daly referenced (briefly) some of the passages cited here.
[194] JFL to McGee, 13 Mar. 1847, NLI, Ms. 340/61.
[195] JFL to Mitchel, 21 Jun. 1847, RIA 12.P.15/7.

latter-day chivalric knights who would "carry her banner in battle".[196] Lalor continued to employ the queen-metaphor in his *Irish Felon* articles, depicting Ireland as "a poor lady" who had been "decrowned" and who must be restored to her rightful position, with "an armed hand" if necessary.[197] "Let us crown her a queen;" Lalor demanded, "and then let her do with her lands as a queen may do."

Lalor never explained his use of such colourful imagery. As discussed in the next chapter, he was keenly interested in the French Revolution of 1789 and its consequences. Perhaps he was influenced by the revolutionaries' depiction of Liberty as a woman named Marianne.[198] However, it is more likely that, in his references to the "island-queen", Lalor was drawing upon the long tradition in Irish literature of personifying the nation in this way. For instance, Gaelic poets of the early-seventeenth century often portrayed Ireland as a female ravaged by a predatory neighbour.[199] Other writers drew on pre-Christian mythology to depict the feminine Ireland in a more assertive light. An example can be found in a popular book listed in the Tinakill catalogue and published in 1843. Described by Quinn as "Young Ireland's most enduring contribution to nationalist literature", it was the most commercially successful of *The Nation's* collections of ballads, entitled appropriately *The Spirit of the Nation*.[200] These lines from a ballad entitled "Western War Song" seem to describe the return of the goddess Ériu, after whom Ireland (or Éire) is named.[201]

> From the rock guarded mountains—her cradle and throne –
> She moves in her splendour—she moves not alone;
> For myriads unsheathing the chain-breaking sword,
> Now hail the bright vision long vainly ador'd.[202]

Similar sentiments can be found in the work of James Clarence Mangan (1803–1849), whose poems, including *Dark Rosaleen*, were published in *The Nation*.

---

[196] *Nation*, 24 Apr. 1847. (Ramón, *JFL*, p. 69.)

[197] *Irish Felon*, 24 Jun. 1848, 8 Jul. 1848 (Ramón, *JFL*, pp. 106, 136.)

[198] Paul R. Hanson, *Historical Dictionary of the French Revolution*, 2nd edn (Lanham, 2015), pp. 211-2.

[199] Joep Leerssen, *Remembrance and Imagination: Patterns in the Historical and Literary Representation of Ireland in the Nineteenth Century* (Cork, 1996), p. 54. For a discussion of the *Aisling* genre in Gaelic poetry, see also Nicholas Williams, "Literature in Irish", in S. J. Connolly (ed.), *The Oxford Companion to Irish History*, 2nd edn (Oxford, 2002).

[200] Quinn, *Young Ireland*, pp. 5, 50.

[201] Patricia Monaghan, *The Encyclopedia of Celtic Mythology and Folklore* (New York, 2004), p. 160.

[202] *The Spirit of the Nation. By the writers of the Nation newspaper*, 2nd edn (Dublin, 1844), p. 50.

The following lines are taken from Mangan's *A cry for Ireland* which appeared in that newspaper in May 1846, just after Lalor returned to Tinakill.

> Oh, my grief... of all griefs
> Is to see...how thy throne
> Is usurped, whilst thy self art in thrall![203]

Lalor's use of the queen-metaphor was uniquely consistent in both his public and private writings of 1847-8. This is remarkable given how *inconsistently* he expressed his position on the more substantial questions of repeal and landholding during the same period. It is therefore appropriate to examine why Lalor felt it necessary to emphasise the queen-metaphor throughout his public career.

In its edition of 15 August 1843, *The Freeman's Journal* devoted eight columns to its report of one of Daniel O'Connell's so-called "monster meetings".[204] According to the reporter, "at least 200,000 persons [were] in attendance" at the gathering which took place near Abbeyleix in Queen's County. In addition to the usual details of attendees and speeches, the article includes several references to tributes made by the assembly to the British monarch. Indeed, the first resolution proposed and passed "with unbounded acclamation" was an expression of Ireland's "devotional allegiance to our beloved sovereign". The speaker who followed O'Connell onto the platform, a land activist named William Conner, claimed that "no true Irishman would change our loved Victoria for all the stern republicans in Europe". At a banquet later that evening attended by O'Connell, the first toast was raised to "the health of the 'Queen'", to which the assembly responded with cries of "God Save the Queen". These expressions of fidelity to Queen Victoria were not confined to meetings of the Repeal Association. In fact, they reflected a tendency within the broad spectrum of Irish nationalism to honour the British crown.[205] In the breakaway Irish Confederation, Thomas D'Arcy McGee was perhaps the most prominent supporter of the royal connection with Britain, a connection so "advantageous" to Ireland, he asserted, that "no sane man will seek to separate".[206] In a lecture on the Irish Constitution delivered in September 1847, McGee drew on historical precedent to argue for the legitimacy of the British monarch's position as Queen of Ireland.[207] Citing the

---

[203] *Nation*, 30 May 1846.
[204] *Freeman's Journal*, 15 Aug. 1843.
[205] James H. Murphy, *Abject Loyalty: Nationalism and Monarchy in Ireland During the Reign of Queen Victoria* (Cork, 2001), pp. xvii-xix..
[206] *Nation*, 16 Oct. 1847.
[207] Ibid., 2 Oct. 1847.

Crown of Ireland Act (1542), McGee claimed that "Queen Victoria now reigns over Ireland".[208] However, even those Young Irelanders at the radical end of the Confederation believed that self-government for Ireland could be reconciled with submission to the British monarchy. The editor of *The Irish Felon*, John Martin, wrote that "I owe no allegiance except to Ireland and to the English Queen, as Queen of Ireland".[209] Michael Doheny was equally firm that "No one questions her Majesty's claim to the crown of Ireland".[210]

It was this almost universal devotion within Irish nationalism to the British monarch that Lalor wished to redirect. Notwithstanding his condemnation of the feudal system of landholding imposed on Ireland, Lalor admired the concept of fealty that was an integral part of medieval feudalism. Along with the act of homage, the oath of fealty required a solemn undertaking by a vassal to defend and protect his lord with honour and chivalry. It created a personal bond between two men, usually a knight and his king. As long as he fulfilled his oath, the vassal was allowed to use the land granted to him by his lord.[211] If he was not already familiar with feudal law, Lalor would have learnt all he needed to know about homage and fealty from the excellent summary in volume two of Blackstone's *Commentaries*.[212] Although long outdated, Lalor saw such merit in this aspect of feudalism that it became a key component of his "new social economy".[213] For anyone to hold land in Lalor's Ireland, he must "bear full, true, and undivided fealty, and allegiance to the nation…"[214] However, if the medieval oath of fealty was made by one person to another, Lalor's adaptation of the feudal code could not apply to an amorphous "nation" or "people". So just as W. B. Yeats did many decades later in his play, *Kathleen Ni Houlihan*, Lalor invoked a potent symbol of Irishness by personifying the nation as a woman. In doing so, he presented royalists in both the nationalist and unionist camps with an allegorical "queen", a "lady paramount", who could supplant their attachment to the British crown.

***

Lalor may have failed to realise his dream of a free Ireland in which landholding was subject to the will of its people. However, he succeeded at least in communicating a number of bold ideas about land tenure and property rights to a wide audience. Unfortunately, the chaos caused by hunger, disease, mass emigration, and rebellion militated against a considered appreciation of the

---

[208] Ibid.
[209] *United Irishman*, 1 Apr. 1848.
[210] *Irish Tribune*, 1 Jul. 1848.
[211] Carl Stephenson, *Mediaeval Feudalism* (Ithaca, 1956), pp. 22-3.
[212] Blackstone, *Commentaries*, ii, pp. 52-8.
[213] *Nation*, 24 Apr. 1847. (Ramón, *JFL*, p. 75.)
[214] *Irish Felon*, 24 Jun. 1848 (Ramón, *JFL*, p. 104.)

vision he outlined. Even if the environment had been less fraught, it is likely that few of his contemporaries would have grasped the radical and farsighted nature of his vision. This is because of Lalor's understandable, if ultimately doomed, strategy of trying to achieve two separate objectives at the same time. By promoting practical steps to alleviate the impact of the Famine, while also articulating his more philosophical principles on property rights, he confused much of his audience. This in turn made it difficult for later scholars of Irish history to appreciate and acknowledge just how far-reaching his thinking on the land question had been. Yet the principles and concepts that were overlooked or misinterpreted by contemporaries and academics became a source of inspiration for subsequent political activists.[215]

As this chapter has argued, James Fintan Lalor outlined a model of landholding that anticipated the ideas of later proponents of land nationalisation. What is more, he linked that model to a form of national self-determination that went beyond the aspirations of the Repeal Association and the Young Ireland movement. As Ramón concluded, Lalor's "seamless combination of agrarian doctrine and popular-sovereignty theory… set Lalor apart [from his contemporaries] and earned him a place of his own in Irish nationalist thought".[216] Nonetheless, before a final judgment can be made as to the uniqueness or innovativeness of Lalor's ideas, a further investigation is needed. Therefore the next chapter will focus on the deliberations of other writers and thinkers on the topics of land tenure and national sovereignty in order to determine what, if any, influence they may have had on Lalor's thinking.

---

[215] James Larkin wrote that "The only two Irishmen I have ever had a regard for were Finton Lawler (sic) and Michael Davitt." (quoted in Donal Nevin, *James Larkin: Lion of the Fold* (Dublin, 1998), p. 140). Éamon de Valera invoked Lalor publicly on several occasions, for instance in his first St. Patrick's Day address just after Fianna Fáil entered government in 1932. (Maurice Moynihan, *Speeches and Statements by Eamon de Valera, 1917-73* (Dublin, 1980), p. 194). Raymond Crotty saw Lalor's teachings as foreshadowing the landholding theories put forward later by Michael Davitt and Henry George. (Raymond Crotty, *Irish Agricultural Production: its Volume and Structure* (Cork, 1966), p. 82).
[216] Ramón, *JFL*, p. 23.

Chapter Two

"Destitute of Books":
Lalor's Literary Precursors

Although he held back from a full expression of his beliefs, at least in public, until "The Faith of a Felon" appeared in print, Lalor seems to have understood from the start how shocking his ideas would seem to others. That much is evident from his first letter to Duffy when he hinted at their revolutionary potential, but did not reveal their substance. It is likely, therefore, that by then Lalor's thinking on landholding was complete in most, if not all, of its radical detail. In "The Faith of a Felon" he maintained that he had recognised the link between nationalism and landholding "years ago". Indeed, Lalor had been thinking about these matters since 1831 according to his unpublished letter "to the landowners of Ireland" written in 1844.[1] The arrival of the potato blight towards the end of 1845, its impact across the Irish countryside, and most especially the response by the ruling classes in Ireland and England, seem to have spurred Lalor into much more radical thinking on both the short and long term implications for his country. Exactly how and when he began to formulate his new theories cannot be ascertained. The extant correspondence, either to or from Lalor, suggests that he started to focus his thoughts on the Famine and the related question of land tenure not long after his return to Tinakill in the spring of 1846. By the time of his first contact with Young Ireland in early January of the following year, he had already discussed his ideas with a friend, John Marnell. Marnell's letters contain the first recorded indications of the impact that Lalor's new thinking had on others, and are discussed in Chapter Three.

The objective of this chapter is to investigate the work of reformers and activists whose ideas are similar to Lalor's. Whether or not any of these influenced Lalor as he developed his doctrines, one thing is abundantly clear. In his thinking on land tenure at any rate, Lalor was not *sui generis*. As this examination of Lalor's literary precursors reveals, he echoed principles and policies that had been aired and discussed long before his articles were published. Nonetheless, by assessing Lalor's proposals on land reform in this wider context, their revolutionary import is only heightened.

---

[1] NLI, Ms. 340/59. (Lalor described himself as "an impartial observer of events in Ireland during the last thirteen years.")

Inspiration and influence

Given his long interest in the land question, Lalor must have read whatever he could on the subject. However being prevented through ill-health from participating in formal education gave him little opportunity to familiarise himself and debate with others the writings on the Irish land question then being disseminated by political economists such as George Poulett Scrope, William Thomas Thornton, and John Stuart Mill.[2] Nevertheless, there is much conjecture in the secondary literature as to the writers whose work may have helped shape Lalor's thinking. Unfortunately, as most scholars either did not delve very deeply into the substance of his theories, or repeated the argument that he favoured either tenant right or peasant proprietorship, such speculation is often misplaced. A typical example is Buckley's assertion that Lalor was "a latter-day physiocrat".[3] This was a reference to a group of eighteenth-century economists in *ancien regime* France, led by François Quesnay.[4] Because Buckley rejected the claim that Lalor advocated land nationalisation, he based his argument on the physiocratic principle that agricultural production was the mainstay of the national economy, a position he rightly associated with Lalor.[5] However, in ignoring the questions of tenure and property rights in his assessment, Buckley overlooked several distinctions between Lalor's doctrines and those of the physiocrats. The most important is Lalor's concept of the people as "first landowners and... lawmakers...", a position that contrasts with the pre-revolutionary monarchical custodianship of the land espoused by Quesnay.[6] Similar examples of inappropriate or unlikely influences can be found in other secondary sources. These include German political economist, Friedrich List,[7] Welsh social reformer, Robert Owen,[8] and Scottish philosopher, Thomas Carlyle.[9] Fogarty was closer to the

---

[2] Peter Gray, "The peculiarities of Irish land tenure, 1800-1914: from agent of impoverishment to agent of pacification", in Donald Norman Winch and Patrick Karl O'Brien (eds.), *The Political Economy of British Historical Experience, 1688-1914* (Oxford, 2002), pp. 145-6.
[3] Buckley, *JFL*, p. 71.
[4] Isaac Kramnick (ed.), *The Portable Enlightenment Reader* (London, 1995), p. 496.
[5] Buckley, *JFL*, pp. 37, 71.
[6] Kramnick, *Enlightenment Reader*, pp. 496-7.
[7] O'Neill, *JFL*, p. 52.
[8] Cathal O'Shannon, "James Fintan Lalor", in M. J. MacManus (ed.), *Thomas Davis and Young Ireland* (Dublin, 1945), pp. 68-70.
[9] Lillian Fogarty, *James Fintan Lalor: Patriot and Political Essayist (1807-1849), with a preface by Arthur Griffith*, ed. John Kelly (Dublin, 1997), p. 14.

mark when she contended that "Wolfe Tone and [Thomas] Davis... moulded Lalor's thought on national and economic questions".[10]

While these supposed influences may merit further investigation, it is impossible to examine each one in the space available. Therefore some preliminary assessment is necessary.[11] Much of that assessment has already been conducted in the previous chapter, i.e. a detailed analysis of Lalor's writings has concluded that, as far as his preferred system of land tenure was concerned, he was a *de facto* nationaliser. Whatever may have been his views on the land question prior to 1846, we are concerned with the new doctrine he unveiled in 1847 and 1848. Consequently, it seems sensible to investigate possible influences by taking that doctrine as the starting point, which virtually all of the historiography fails to do.

Of course, land tenure is but one of two elements in Lalor's principal doctrine, the other being Irish independence. The link between the two is encapsulated in his phrase, "like a railway carriage to the engine". In the case of the first element, land tenure, he proposed a radical departure from the accepted norm of individual property rights. His policy on the national question was less remarkable. While Lalor went beyond the aspirations of contemporary nationalist thinking, his goal of full independence was in line with the objectives of the United Irishmen and Robert Emmet rebellions, both of which occurred within living memory. As Lalor reminded Duffy and the other Confederation leaders, the pre-1800 regime that they sought to restore "was the very form of connection which TONE and LORD EDWARD died to repeal — as well as many others beside..."[12] So the truly revolutionary aspect of Lalor's teachings was not his invocation of a republican tradition that predated the Act of Union, it was his concept of land as a communal resource that should never be circumscribed by an individual landowner. As discussed in the next chapter, for many of his readers and listeners in late-1840s Ireland, that was not only incomprehensible, it was unthinkable.

Viewed from that perspective, Lalor was unique among his peers and associates in Ireland during the first half of the nineteenth century. When looked at in a broader context of space and time, however, what he proposed was not so startling. Indeed, his theories on the land question echoed longstanding philosophical and legal concepts that had been discussed and

---

[10] Fogarty, *JFL*, pp. xix-xx. Davis' writings on land tenure are discussed below.
[11] Other possible influences on Lalor's land policy examined for this book, and eliminated from further consideration, include James Hope (1764–1847), William Thompson (1775-1833), and William Blacker (1776–1850).
[12] *Irish Felon*, 1 Jul. 1848. (Ramón, *JFL*, pp. 122-3.)

argued about for centuries. In his survey of the major theorists of property from the early seventeenth century up to the eve of Chartism, Thomas Horne explored the question of individual versus communal rights as they were developed and debated during the period.[13] He argued that thinkers such as Hugo Grotius (1583-1645), Thomas Hobbes (1588-1679), and Samuel von Pufendorf (1632-1694) agreed, despite their other differences, that the concepts of natural law and individual property rights could be reconciled. In other words, although they believed that God granted the earth to all mankind, they accepted that owners of property held the right to exclude others from its use.[14] As Grotius wrote

> For as soon as living in common was no longer approved of, all men were supposed, and ought to be supposed to have consented, that each should appropriate to himself, by right of first possession, what could not have been divided.[15]

Grotius and his successors were concerned with establishing principles of law that would govern the increasingly complex societies in which they lived. However, those principles were criticised by later generations of radical thinkers who, from the middle of the eighteenth century, began to promote alternative forms of land tenure that recognised the community's claim on privately-held land. By the 1830s and 1840s, therefore, when Lalor became interested in the Irish land question, there was a considerable body of published material in English, whether academic or political in origin, dealing with the principles of property in land. How much of these writings Lalor was aware of, or had access to, is unknown. Yet, in order to appreciate and assess his theories on landholding, it is necessary to look beyond the narrow confines of Irish nationalist history, and explore the intellectual context in which he formulated and propounded those theories.

Acquiring "pure English"

As stated above, Lalor began to think about the Irish land question in 1831 when he was 24 years old. His published writings provide a few clues as to the people, organisations, and events he either admired, or of which he was at least aware. Insofar as any of these references related to the land question, the

---

[13] Thomas A. Horne, *Property Rights and Poverty: Political Argument in Britain, 1605-1834* (London, 1990).
[14] Ibid., p. 10.
[15] Hugo Grotius, *The Rights of War and Peace* (London, 1738), pp. 145-6. (Quoted in Horne, *Property Rights*, p. 13.)

possibility of influence cannot be discounted. In addition, his brother Richard compiled a catalogue of books held in Tinakill after he inherited their father's property in the late-1850s.[16] It is likely that many of these books were available during James Fintan's life and some may be relevant to this enquiry. As to what Lalor may have read outside Tinakill, there are some hints in the limited archive.

That Lalor loved reading is clear from the testimony of his friends. Yet he complained that "I have all my life been destitute of books".[17] Luby reminisced many years later about his friend's literary interests:

> Though without a regular college education, he possessed considerable scholarship; he knew something of the ancient classics (Latin, at all events, he knew fairly); and if the range of his general reading was not very wide, it was certainly above the average. Whatever he did read, he probably read with great care and thought.[18]

It is impossible to reconstruct Lalor's reading history to determine what may have influenced the direction of his thinking on land. The sources indicate that he was a voracious consumer of books and newspapers when they were available to him but, given that he spent most of his life in rural isolation with limited access to reading material, his *cri de coeur* is easy to understand. Lalor's interests encompassed popular fiction by writers such as Walter Scott and William Wordsworth, as well as those political and philosophical works that came his way.[19] Because of his lifelong poor health, Lalor had only one year of formal education at Carlow College during his late teens. For much of his brief time as a boarder at the school, recurring illness meant that he was often confined to his room and seldom if ever attended class.[20] Instead, according to the reminiscences of a former school friend, Maurice Lenihan, the bed-ridden Lalor spent his days poring over the writings of Henry St John, first Viscount Bolingbroke, while taking notes as he read. According to Lenihan, it was the author's "style" that appealed to Lalor.[21] This suggests that Lalor was more interested in the language and syntax of what he read, rather than in the substance of Bolingbroke's arguments and opinions. These, as far as the land question is concerned, reflected mainstream assumptions about individual property rights and the superior status of the

---

[16] NLI, Ms. 8570/02.
[17] *Irish Felon*, 8 Jul. 1848 (Ramón, *JFL*, p. 137.)
[18] *Irish Nation*, 17 Dec. 1881.
[19] Ibid., 1 Apr. 1882.
[20] *Tipperary Vindicator*, 26 Apr., 30 Apr. 1867.
[21] Ibid., 30 Apr. 1867.

landowning class.²² Nonetheless Lalor's early reading of Bolingbroke made a lasting impression on his literary style. In a tribute to his former associate at *The Irish Felon*, Joseph Brenan remarked of Lalor that he "wrote pure English—purer than the English of Bolingbroke, who was his model".²³ It is clear from Luby's memoirs that Lalor enjoyed great writing, irrespective of the political leanings of the author. Luby recalled that his friend was impressed by the "logical power" he found in the works of two very different thinkers: the radical philosopher Jeremy Bentham and the conservative Catholic bishop, John Milner.²⁴ Fiction enthralled Lalor also. He revelled in argumentative discussions about the writings of poets and novelists such as Milton, Wordsworth and Scott.²⁵ Finally, Luby also alluded to his friend's pride in the literary qualities of his own *Nation* and *Irish Felon* articles and his dismay at how few of his contemporaries appreciated "the finer features of the[ir] composition".²⁶

These anecdotes suggest that Lalor learnt *how* to write from the books he read, but they are silent on the question of whether or not these, or other sources, also informed *what* he wrote. All that can be stated with any confidence is that Lalor was sufficiently literate and interested to have read any book, pamphlet, or newspaper article on the question of property in land that he could lay his hands on. For instance, as is described below, he undoubtedly came across the ideas of John Locke. However, Locke argued in favour of individual rights of property and inheritance.²⁷ As indicated above, there was also a body of published opinion that challenged those rights and which, because of its similarities to Lalor's ideas, is worth exploring.

British radicals and land tenure

Much of the contemporary literature on the subject of property in land was written by British authors. This reflected a deep concern by a variety of commentators and observers in the neighbouring island about the respective rights of landowners and tenants. As stated in the previous chapter, the Devon Commission identified a number of historical factors that resulted in the system of landholding in Ireland

---

²² H.T. Dickinson, *Bolingbroke* (London, 1970), pp. 171-2, 311.
²³ *Irishman*, 16 Mar. 1850.
²⁴ *Irish Nation*, 17 Dec. 1881. According to Luby, Lalor was interested in Bentham's discussion of usury laws. Although Bentham was involved in reform of the land laws, he did not question individual property rights. (see Mary Sokol, "Jeremy Bentham and the real property commission of 1828", *Utilitas*, 4/2 (1992), pp. 225-45.)
²⁵ *Irish Nation*, 1 Apr. 1882.
²⁶ Ibid., 28 Jan. 1882.
²⁷ Horne, *Property Rights*, pp. 48-65.

evolving differently from that in Britain. The report cited confiscation and colonisation of Irish land, fuelled by religious conflict, as the principal causes of the differences between the two countries. The commission made only passing reference to the British land system, merely stating that over time feudalism was gradually replaced by "the more civilised relation of landlord and tenant, as known to our present law".[28] However, Lord Devon's bland summary left out an important development in British legal history which, while it may not have been as disruptive as the various land issues afflicting Ireland, brought about significant social change. This was the enclosure of land hitherto regarded by local people as communal property and used by them for grazing cattle and growing crops.[29] The process of transferring common land to individual ownership had been going on since the Middle Ages (not without resistance by groups such as the Diggers).[30] By 1750 "possibly half the land of England had been enclosed".[31] After 1750, individual landowners increasingly petitioned parliament to allow them to expropriate common land without the consent of those who had previously used it. From then until about 1830, it is estimated that a further 20% of England's land, or more than 6,000,000 acres, was enclosed under parliamentary legislation.[32] The consolidation of land into larger farms facilitated the development and application of more efficient farming methods, but it also displaced many thousands of smallholders and peasants. If they were to survive, they had little choice but to become paid labourers, whether in field or factory.[33] As one modern scholar has put it, "The break-up of the peasantry was the price England paid for the increased supplies of corn and meat to feed her growing population".[34]

Although not as widespread, enclosure of common lands also occurred in parts of Ireland during the eighteenth century.[35] From time to time this was met with violent protest, e.g. the Whiteboy movement that emerged in some Irish

---

[28] *Parl. Paps.* (1845), XXVIII. [1], pp. 6-7.
[29] Gordon E. Mingay, *Parliamentary Enclosure in England: an Introduction to its Causes, Incidence and Impact 1750-1850* (London, 1997), pp. 7-8.
[30] E. Eldon Barry, *Nationalisation in British Politics: the Historical Background* (London, 1965), pp. 19-22.
[31] Peter Mathias, *The First Industrial Nation: an Economic History of Britain 1700-1914* (London, 1983), p. 56.
[32] Jerome Blum, "English parliamentary enclosure", *Journal of Modern History*, 53/3, Sep. 1981, pp. 477-504.
[33] Mathias, *First Industrial Nation*, pp. 54-5.
[34] Ibid., p. 56.
[35] John Chapman, "The extent and nature of parliamentary enclosure", *Agricultural History Review*, 35/1, 1987, pp. 25-35, fn 7. F. H. A. Aalen, "Enclosures in eastern Ireland. A general introduction", *Irish Geography*, 5/2, 1965, pp. 30-5.

counties.³⁶ In England, in the main, the application of parliamentary enclosures precipitated a literary response in the form of pamphlets and newspaper articles arguing for or against the practice. The literature that developed is considerable and too vast to explore in this chapter. What can be said is that, while many opponents of enclosure put pen to paper to express their views, very few questioned the system that allowed a small number of wealthy individuals to expand their landholdings at the expense of their less fortunate neighbours.³⁷ However, a handful of contemporary commentators went further and argued for a fundamental reappraisal of the rights of property in land. Although their perspectives differed in certain details, from each other and from Lalor's own proposals, they all shared his principle that the community should play a greater role in the disposition of land, even at the expense of individual rights. While Lalor probably never read any of these publications, his magpie mind was alert enough to have absorbed the essential ideas, should he have come across them in newspapers or through his interactions with friends and acquaintances.³⁸ Whether or not they exerted any direct influence on Lalor's thinking, the writers discussed below were, like him, at odds with the society in which they lived insofar as their views on land tenure are concerned.

William Ogilvie

In his comprehensive survey of the history of nationalisation in Britain, E. Eldon Barry nominated Professor William Ogilvie (1736-1819) of King's College, Aberdeen as having written "the first theoretical criticism of private landowning".³⁹ Barry was referring to a book published anonymously in London in 1781.⁴⁰ As a respected classical scholar, Ogilvie presumably did not want his reputation to be tarnished by association with the ideas in his book

---

[36] Barry, *Nationalisation in British politics*, p. 22. James S. Donnelly, "The Whiteboy movement, 1761-5", *IHS*, 21/81, Mar. 1978, pp. 21-6.

[37] S. J. Thompson, "Parliamentary enclosure, property, population, and the decline of classical republicanism in eighteenth-century Britain", *The Historical Journal*, 51/3, Sep. 2008, pp. 621-42

[38] The archive contains several written testimonials which attest to Lalor's intellectual curiosity and capability, e.g. "His mind I regard as clear, practical and conceptive, marked with strength and originality and well stored with acquirements of the highest and most useful order." (W. N. Walshe, MD, 8 Oct. 1845, NLI, Ms 340/162).

[39] Barry, *Nationalisation in British politics*, p. 23.

[40] William Ogilvie, *An Essay on the Right of Property in Land: with respect to its foundation in the law of nature, its present establishment by the municipal laws of Europe, and the regulations by which it might be rendered more beneficial to the lower ranks of mankind* (London, 1781).

and so he did not identify himself as the author. In the introduction, Ogilvie revealed that he had been questioning in his mind "for some years past" the principles underlining property in land that prevailed throughout Europe.[41] As the extended title of his book indicates, the focus of Ogilvie's enquiry was to see how the present system could be improved to make it "more beneficial to the lower ranks of mankind".

Ogilvie began his treatise with a declaration that foreshadowed Lalor's own central principle:

> The earth having been given to mankind in common occupancy, each individual seems to have by nature a right to possess and cultivate an equal share. That right is little different from that which he has to the free use of the open air and running water.[42]

If the earth was meant to be a natural resource like air and water available to all, the reality "in most countries in Europe", Ogilvie maintained, was quite different. Again, Lalor would have concurred with Ogilvie's condemnation of "that exclusive right to the improvable value of the soil, which a few men, never in any country exceeding one-hundredth part of the community are permitted to engross..."[43] Ogilvie went on to denounce the "exorbitant rents" and "short leases" which landlords imposed on their tenants.[44] His solution was a "progressive Agrarian law" that would grant smallholders security of tenure in the form of a long lease, "sufficient at least for the farmer to bring up his family...", and a rent "fixed at a determined proportion... of the annual produce of the soil".[45] Like Lalor more than a half-century later, Ogilvie argued that it was in the best long-term interests of the aristocracy to foster national unity by acquiescing in the creation of a more equitable land system, "though at the expense of diminishing in some degree the privileges and emoluments of their own order".[46] Even so, according to Ogilvie, it would probably require an all-powerful ruler to drive change from the top.[47] Ogilvie cited three precedents in European history where sovereigns had instituted a radical redistribution of land: Henry VIII's dissolution of the monasteries in Britain, the Cromwellian land confiscations in Ireland, and Phillip III's expulsion of the "Moors" from Spain. Ogilvie's only

---

[41] Ibid., pp. iii-iv.
[42] Ibid., pp. 11-12.
[43] Ibid., p. 37.
[44] Ibid., p. 38.
[45] Ibid., pp. 89-90.
[46] Ibid., pp. 104-5.
[47] Ibid., p. 141.

criticism of these upheavals was that, had the instigators followed his "law", they would have ensured a more equitable division of the spoils between "the courtiers and grandees" on the one hand, and the "cultivators" on the other.[48]

Ogilvie believed that a similar, but less drastic, initiative by a present-day ruler could bring about the reform he advocated. He recommended that change be introduced gradually and with due consultation, so that those affected understood and supported the rationale behind the reform.[49] Under his proposed regime, the end result would be that "every individual who would choose it, should be the proprietor of a field, and employed in its cultivation..."[50] However, unlike Lalor, Ogilvie was not concerned about the rest of society whose members, as far as farming the land was concerned, had neither opportunity nor interest, but who depended for their very existence on its produce. There would be no transfers of rent to the general community for the benefit of all citizens, as Lalor proposed. Ogilvie's plan began and ended in the countryside and involved nothing more than greater equity between landlord and tenant, of the kind promoted later in Ireland by the Repeal Association and its allies. Ogilvie had inherited a landed estate from his parents and was not predisposed to lobby for property rights to be overthrown completely.[51] He wanted a fairer system—not a revolution. This is clear from his attitude to the enclosing of common land which, if it discommoded the peasantry, also benefited landowners through higher rents and greater efficiency.[52] He was not against the practice—he simply wanted it carried out in a more equitable manner.[53]

Allan has argued that Ogilvie's stance on the question of land as property was "at odds" with the views of his better-known contemporaries, Adam Smith and Adam Ferguson.[54] In the context of eighteenth-century Scottish philosophical

---

[48] Ibid., pp. 93-5.
[49] Ibid., pp. 96-7.
[50] Ibid., p. 33.
[51] Lionel Alexander Ritchie, "Ogilvie, William (1736–1819), classical scholar and advocate of common property in land." *ODNB*,
(http://ezproxy-prd.bodleian.ox.ac.uk:2167/view/10.1093/ref:odnb/9780198614128.001.0001/odnb-9780198614128-e-20589) 3 Mar. 2018.
[52] Mingay, *Parliamentary Enclosure in England*, pp. 20, 83.
[53] Ogilvie, *Right of Property in Land*, p. 223.
[54] David Allan, "'The wisest and most beneficial schemes': William Ogilvie, radical political economy and the Scottish Enlightenment", in Gordon Pentland & Michael T Davis (eds.), *Liberty, Property and Popular Politics: England and Scotland, 1688-1815 : Essays in Honour of H.T. Dickinson* (Edinburgh, 2016), p. 110.

thought, Allan's case for Ogilvie as being willing to stretch the limits of acceptable intellectual discourse is well made. Barry summed up Ogilvie's contribution:

> Ogilvie's scheme was not so radical as at first appears… All the same, the mere suggestion that Government should interfere with the system of large estates was daring enough in its time. [55]

Thomas Spence

Ogilvie's identity as the author of *An Essay on the Right of Property in Land* was revealed many years after his death when his views became topical following the success of Henry George's *Progress and Poverty*.[56] At the time of publication, however, few people were aware of Ogilvie's authorship and the book itself drew little notice.[57] It did come to the attention, of Thomas Spence (1750-1814), a book-seller from Newcastle upon Tyne who developed his own radical ideas about landholding and property rights.[58] Like Ogilvie, Spence was of Scottish extraction but there the similarities ended. Spence came from a poor background and was largely self-educated.[59] Unlike Ogilvie, he proclaimed his views on land reform publicly and repeatedly, leading to several spells in prison.[60] Spence's legacy, in Barry's estimation, lies in his being "the first radical to propose public ownership of all land on principle".[61] Spence's interest in landed property rights was aroused by a civil dispute that erupted in Newcastle when he was a young man. In 1771 the town's corporation tried to enclose 89 acres of common land which had hitherto been available to Newcastle's citizens. A legal battle ensued which the corporation lost. As a result of this episode, Spence decided that what he termed "the overbearing power of great men [made them] dangerous companions in society". He began to think about how society could be reformed to render it more equitable.[62] An opportunity to communicate his ideas presented itself four years later when he was invited to

---

[55] Barry, *Nationalisation in British politics*, p. 24.
[56] J. Morrison Davidson, *Concerning Four Precursors of Henry George and the Single Tax* (London, 1899), pp. 3-4.
[57] James Eayrs, "The political ideas of the English agrarians, 1775-1815", *Canadian Journal of Economics and Political Science*, 18/3, Aug. 1952, p. 295.
[58] Olive Durant Rudkin, *Thomas Spence and his Connections* (London, 1927), p. 17.
[59] H. T. Dickinson, "Spence, Thomas (1750–1814), radical and bookseller", *ODNB*. (http://ezproxy-prd.bodleian.ox.ac.uk:2167/view/10.1093/ref:odnb/9780198614128.001.0001/odnb-9780198614128-e-26112) 15 Jan. 2018.
[60] Horne, *Property Rights*, p. 219.
[61] Barry, *Nationalisation in British Politics*, p. 25.
[62] Rudkin, *Thomas Spence*, pp. 26-7.

present a paper at the recently-formed Newcastle Philosophical Society. The original paper is lost but Spence reprinted it in pamphlet form in 1793 under the title *The Rights of Man*.[63]

According to this source, Spence opened his lecture by proclaiming that:

> The country of any people, in a native state, is properly their common, in which each of them has an equal property, with free liberty to sustain himself and connections with the animals, fruits, and other products thereof.[64]

However, Spence asserted, this original order was subverted by "a few" [...who...] divided [the land] among themselves... as if they had manufactured it".[65] "Thus", Spence concluded, "were the first land-holders usurpers and tyrants; and all who have since possessed their lands, have done so by right of inheritance, purchase, etc. from them".[66] The consequence for the rest of mankind, according to Spence, was that they "may not live in any part of the world, not even where they are born but as strangers and by the permission of the pretender to the property thereof..."[67] In order to rectify this imbalance, Spence outlined a plan to bring about radical societal change. In contrast to Ogilvie's "top-down" approach, Spence's reform would spring, not from the will of an omnipotent ruler, but from the collective resolution of "the whole people in some country... that every man has an equal property in the land in the neighbourhood where he resides". Implementation of this principle would be devolved to the citizens of individual parishes with the power to take possession of "the land with all that appertains to it" from the existing landholders.[68] Rent, formerly paid to the landlords, would instead be divided between central government and the local parishes. Spence went on to delineate the uses to which each parish would put its share of the land revenue, e.g. relief of poverty, infrastructure renewal, civil defence, etc.[69] Given this parish focus, Spence saw no need for a large national administration. Moreover,

---

[63] Thomas Spence, *The Rights of Man, as exhibited in a lecture, read at the Philosophical Society, in Newcastle*, 4th ed. (London, 1793).
[64] Ibid., p. 5.
[65] Ibid., p. 8.
[66] Ibid., p. 9.
[67] Ibid., p. 10.
[68] Ibid., pp. 11-12.
[69] Ibid., pp. 12-13.

he envisaged that the revenue collected, and largely dispensed, at parish level would be sufficient to obviate the need for any other tolls or taxes.[70]

Spence's ideas were closer to Lalor's thinking than Ogilvie's proposed new law. Spence anticipated Lalor's concept of land as a public resource rather than a private asset in the hands of a few. Both men also believed that societal change should develop through the formation of local bodies, i.e. Spence's parish corporations or Lalor's tenant leagues and trade associations. Through these means the people would secure control of the land, and all land users would hold their properties as tenants of the people. The rents they paid would be used to fund the services required by the nation's citizens.[71] Lalor believed that, for his plan to work, Ireland must free itself from Westminster rule and be governed by a National Council acknowledged and accepted by the people of Ireland.[72] Although not a nationalist in either the English or Irish sense, Spence too rejected elitist central rule in favour of the popular will, although he placed greater weight on local autonomy than Lalor did. As demonstrated in the previous chapter, Lalor's views about land and property were too extreme for many of his contemporaries. Spence, too, was marginalised, even in radical circles, because of his opposition to individual property rights.[73]

Initially, both reformers hoped that the radical changes they advocated could be accomplished through reason and persuasion. As described in Chapter One, up to and including the Holy Cross meeting in September 1847, Lalor adopted a conciliatory approach to the landlords in line with the Confederation strategy of maintaining their goodwill. By the following summer, however, he was calling publicly for "the English garrison of landlords [to be] instantly expelled".[74] Spence's attitude towards the landowners changed also, though not as precipitately as Lalor's apparent *volte face*. Beginning with his first public lecture in 1775, Spence outlined how the implementation of his plan would be preceded by "much reasoning and deliberation".[75] As late as 1793, he envisaged that landlords could "subsist comfortably" on the "money and moveable effects" they

---

[70] Ibid., pp. 17-18.
[71] Given Spence's earlier conception of this idea, he has been judged by a Marxist journalist to have been "the author of "Single Tax', which was advocated a century later by Henry George". (Max Beer, *The Pioneers of Land Reform: Thomas Spence, William Ogilvie, Thomas Paine* (London, 1920), p. vii.)
[72] *Nation*, 5 Jun. 1847. (Ramón, *JFL*, pp. 89-92.)
[73] Thomas R. Knox, "Thomas Spence: The Trumpet of Jubilee", *Past & Present*, /76, Aug. 1977, p. 92.
[74] *Irish Felon*, 1 Jul. 1848 (Ramón, *JFL*, p. 110.)
[75] Spence, *Rights of Man*, p. 11.

could retain when their property was confiscated.[76] Two years later, however, Spence's tone had hardened. In another pamphlet published in 1795, he warned of a "war" between the people and the aristocracy, should the latter "contend the matter", resulting in "the People... destroying them Root and Branch".[77] The catalyst for Spence's change of heart was the French Revolution, which, by 1795, had led to the dispossession, exile, or killing of many thousands of nobles and other supposed enemies of the new rulers. His isolation, even among his fellow-radicals, was only exacerbated by his continued support of the bloody events unfolding in France. As one scholar has noted,

> It was typical of Spence that his francophilia flourished at a time when nearly all of his country-men hated, feared, or were indifferent to the French Revolution.[78]

Thomas Paine

Another defender of the French Revolution was Thomas Paine (1737-1809), whose writings Spence knew well. In January 1793, Spence was arrested and imprisoned for selling copies of Paine's 1791 book, *Rights of Man* from his book-stall in London.[79] Paine was a hugely successful author whose political and philosophical books and pamphlets sold in their hundreds of thousands in America and Europe. He supported both the American and French revolutions and participated in the government administrations set up in each country following the overthrow of the previous regimes.[80] Spence undoubtedly supported Paine's attack on landowning aristocrats in the second part of his *Rights of Man*:

> The aristocracy are not the farmers who work the land, and raise the produce, but are the mere consumers of the rent; and when compared with the active world, are the drones, a seraglio of males, who neither collect the honey nor form the hive, but exist only for lazy enjoyment.[81]

---

[76] Ibid., pp. 30-1.
[77] Ibid., pp. 8-9.
[78] T. M. Parssinen, "Thomas Spence and the origins of English land nationalization", *Journal of the History of Ideas*, 34/1, Jan- Mar. 1973, p. 138.
[79] *Evening Mail*, 14 Jan. 1793. *Lloyd's Evening Post*, Feb. 25, 1793.
[80] Mark Philp, "Paine, Thomas (1737–1809), author and revolutionary", *ODNB* (http://ezproxy-prd.bodleian.ox.ac.uk:2167/view/10.1093/ref:odnb/9780198614128.001.0001/odnb-9780198614128-e-21133) 21 Jan. 2018.
[81] Thomas Paine, *Rights of Man. Part the second.* (Carlisle, 1792), p. 61

Paine's criticism reflected his antipathy towards the British House of Lords whose members ensured that they, through the legislative power they wielded, paid proportionately less tax than other sectors of society.[82] However, unlike Spence, he was not prepared to advocate that their lands be seized and redistributed to the wider community.

In 1796 Paine outlined his land programme in greater detail in a pamphlet entitled *Agrarian Justice*. His statement of principle "that the earth, in its natural uncultivated state, was, and ever would have continued to be, the COMMON PROPERTY OF THE HUMAN RACE" chimed with the similar sentiments expressed by Ogilvie, Spence, and the later proponents of public control such as Lalor and Henry George.[83] However Paine also accepted that individual, exclusive ownership was the system that now prevailed and, while he wished to reform that system, he would not find any fault with the landowners whose property rights he defended.[84] In 1846 Lalor interpreted the Famine as a revolutionary event that offered an opportunity to transform Irish society by creating a new system of landholding. A half-century earlier, an actual revolution (in France) seemed to Paine to present a similar opportunity for land reform in Britain, one designed to bring about greater equity between the "landed monopoly" and the "dispossessed".[85] Paine proposed that a tax, or what he called a "ground-rent", be levied at an average rate of 13% on all transfers of landed property made as a result of inheritance. Under Paine's plan, the liability would fall upon the heirs "without diminishing or deranging the property of the present possessors".[86] Part of the funds collected would be disbursed in annual pensions of 10 pounds to the old and disabled. In addition, all citizens would receive a once-off payment of 15 pounds upon reaching the age of 21. Paine made no distinction between rich and poor but, in his calculations, he assumed that wealthy citizens would forgo their entitlements.[87] British historian E. P. Thompson wrote that Paine was not disturbed by the unequal distribution of wealth throughout society. Paine's target was *inherited* wealth and privilege and that is why, according to Thompson, "he did not challenge the property-rights of the rich nor the

---

[82] Ibid., p. 60.
[83] Thomas Paine, *Agrarian Justice, opposed to agrarian law, and to agrarian monopoly* (London, 1797), p. 12.
[84] Ibid., pp. 14, 16. Paine became a landlord himself on his American property. (see J. C. D. Clark, *Thomas Paine: Britain, America, and France in the Age of Enlightenment and Revolution* (Oxford, 2018), p. 394.)
[85] Ibid., p. 15.
[86] Ibid., pp. 16-17.
[87] Ibid., pp. 23-4.

doctrines of *laissez-faire*.[88] Paine wrote *Agrarian Justice* while living in revolutionary France and his plan did not conflict with the property rights upheld by the Directory and protected by the various national constitutions introduced since 1789.[89] While many millions of hectares of French land were nationalised following confiscations from the Church and the landowning *émigrés*, the new state quickly sold this land to middle-class and peasant citizens in order to replenish the national finances.[90]

If this outcome disappointed Spence, so too did Paine's latest pamphlet. As he was writing a pamphlet of his own, Spence read *Agrarian Justice* and decided to add to the new publication his own "Strictures" on Paine's proposal. Firstly, though, Spence welcomed Paine's acceptance of the principle that mankind held the earth in common, especially as Paine's "celebrity will procure him many readers". He then went on to express his dissatisfaction with the "contemptible and insulting" provisions which Paine offered as a means of restoring some equity to the landless.[91] In an appendix to his pamphlet, Spence outlined 20 points of difference between *Agrarian Justice* and his own land programme. In his fourteenth point, he asserted that Paine would have existing landowners live among the people "as a distinct and separate body... in full possession of their country". If Spence's plan were implemented, on the other hand, landowners "must either submit to become indistinguishable in the general mass of citizens or fly the country".[92]

Of the three writers examined thus far, Ogilvie, Spence and Paine, Spence was unquestionably closest in his thinking to James Fintan Lalor. However, it is also the case that Spence's radical proposals never attained the levels of circulation and support achieved by, as Horne characterised them, "Paine's more moderate reforms".[93] Sales of Paine's best-known works, *Common Sense* and *Rights of Man*, exceeded 100,000 and his books and pamphlets were reprinted and translated throughout the western world.[94] Given his reputation as "the most famous theoretical critic in these times", it is no surprise that Paine's writings were widely

---

[88] E. P. Thompson, *The Making of the English Working Class* (New York, 1963), pp. 95-6.
[89] Colin Jones, *The Longman Companion to the French Revolution* (Harlow, 1988), pp. 65-72.
[90] Noelle Plack, "The peasantry, feudalism, and the environment, 1789-93", in Peter McPhee (ed.), *A Companion to the French Revolution* (Somerset, 2012), pp. 219-21.
[91] Thomas Spence, *The Rights of Infants* (London, 1797), p. 3.
[92] Ibid., pp. 13-4.
[93] Horne, *Property rights*, p. 223.
[94] Jack Fruchtman Jr., "Foreword", in Sidney Hook (ed.), *Common Sense, Rights of Man, and Other Essential Writings of Thomas Paine* (New York, 2003), p. vii.

read in Ireland.[95] All 10,000 copies of his *Rights of Man* published in Ireland in 1791 were sold in a matter of months, despite the decision by several newspapers to print extensive extracts from the work during the same period.[96] An Irish printing of *Agrarian Justice* appeared shortly after its original publication in London and it was also serialised in the short-lived United Irishman newspaper, *Press*.[97] According to Dickson, Paine's polemical writings made a significant impact in Irish radical circles in the years leading up to the 1798 rebellion.[98] Spence, on the other hand, does not seem to have found a sympathetic printer or newspaper editor in Ireland to transmit his ideas there.[99] They gained some exposure, however, shortly after Spence's death in 1814. Later that same year a number of his admirers formed the Society of Spencean Philanthropists to promote his plan for collective ownership at the parish level.[100] In 1817 the activities of this group were reported in the Irish and British press following a riot in which they were involved.[101] The Irish coverage included some fleeting references to Spence's land programme, but these offered no substantial detail and received little prominence in the newspaper.[102] Although two biographical pamphlets were published in England after his death, Spence's radical ideas made little or no impact in Ireland and it is unlikely that Lalor ever chanced upon them.[103]

The United Irishmen

In contrast, as Dickson has argued, Paine exerted considerable influence on the United Irishmen.[104] Indeed, traces of Paine's thinking on the land question can be detected in the writings of two of that organisation's leading members,

---

[95] Barry, *Nationalisation in British politics*, p. 25.
[96] David Dickson, "Paine and Ireland", in David Dickson, Daire Keogh and Kevin Whelan (eds.), *The United Irishmen: Republicanism, Radicalism and Rebellion* (Dublin, 1993), p. 138.
[97] Ibid., p. 147.
[98] Ibid., p. 149.
[99] One of the very few mentions of Spence in the Irish press appeared when *The Freeman's Journal*, (16, Apr. 1801) carried *The Times* article announcing his arrest for selling one of his own pamphlets.
[100] Rudkin, *Thomas Spence*, p. 144.
[101] Ibid., pp. 155-6.
[102] *Freeman's Journal*, 3 Mar. 1817, 25 Jun. 1817.
[103] Thomas Evans, *A Brief Sketch of the Life of Mr. Thomas Spence* (Manchester, 1821). Allen Davenport, *The Life, Writings, and Principles of Thomas Spence* (London, 1836). Cited in Barry, *Nationalisation in British Politics*, pp. 25 (fn. 34), 27 (fn. 42).
[104] Dickson, "Paine and Ireland", pp. 140-1.

Thomas Russell (1767-1803) and Arthur O'Connor (1763-1852).[105] Both men published their views on the inequalities of contemporary society as they saw them, one of which was the concentration of landownership in the hands of a few. However, like Paine, neither proposed that the current system be overturned or radically reformed. Russell affirmed the principle pronounced by so many others before and since that "the earth was given to man by he who alone had a right to give it, for his subsistence". Nonetheless, although he seemed to accept the entitlement of all to the land, Russell also wrote that "It is not here intended to question the right of landed property",[106] In his more substantial reflection on the same questions, O'Connor reiterated Paine's analysis of the origins of property in land:

> In the early and barbarous ages of Europe, the only property which was in existence, was the spontaneous productions of the earth; and when lands were monopolized, all power was monopolized also.[107]

For O'Connor, the way to break that monopoly was to divide large estates among many small proprietors. This was happening in France following the Revolution, with the result that the country was "every day approaching nearer to a state of repose and security..."[108] It is hardly surprising that Russell and O'Connor echoed Paine's goal of extending individual property rights to the masses, rather than seeking to undermine those rights. As Blackshields and Considine contended in their analysis of O'Connor's pamphlet, he and his associates were engaged in an effort to adapt "the ideas and events from revolutionary America and France... to fit the Irish context".[109] In both countries, the new regimes upheld property rights.

As stated in Chapter One, in his nationalist aspirations Lalor looked to the United Irishmen for inspiration. On the land question, however, the principles articulated in pamphlets and articles by that organisation's leaders fell short of the proposals that he would espouse in his *Irish Felon* articles. Even the most revolutionary examples of nationalist thinking on this question did not

---

[105] Tony Moore, "Citizens of the world: Paine and the political prisoners transported to Australia", in Sam Edwards and Marcus Morris (eds.), *The Legacy of Thomas Paine in the Transatlantic World* (Abingdon, 2017), p. 161.

[106] Thomas Russell, *A Letter to the People of Ireland, on the present situation of the country* (Belfast, 1796), p. 17.

[107] Arthur O'Connor, *The State of Ireland*, 2nd edn (London, 1798), pp. 45-6.

[108] Ibid., p. 76.

[109] Daniel Blackshields and John Considine, "Economic thought in Arthur O'Connor's "The State of Ireland": reducing politics to science", in Boylan and Prendergast, *History of Irish Economic Thought*, pp. 84-5.

advocate anything as sweeping as Spence's proposed overhaul of the land system. In his examination of Irish radicalism during the late-eighteenth century, Smyth singled out an 11-page pamphlet, apparently written shortly before the 1798 rebellion by a supporter or member of the United Irishmen, as "even more radical than Paine".[110] The anonymous author declared his belief "in the natural and imprescriptible rights of all citizens to all the land". In the next sentence, he outlined how his principle should be put into effect:

> I believe the soil, nor any part of it, cannot be transferred without the consent of the people, or their representatives, convened and authorised, by the votes of every man having arrived at the age of twenty one years...[111]

Although the author was not suggesting any form of land nationalisation or communal ownership, his proposal regarding land transfers went considerably beyond Paine's proposed inheritance tax. Moreover, in assigning control of this aspect of landholding to the "people", he anticipated a key aspect of Lalor's later doctrine. Although Smyth acknowledged this pamphlet as "an extraordinary document", he also argued that it is "not quite the proto-socialist manifesto it might at first appear". This is because the aspiration of the anonymous author for the land to be redistributed was based on his desire to restore ownership to those families dispossessed by the English plantations.[112] In other words, he was more concerned about addressing individual historic grievances than in instituting a new form of popular control over land tenures. Such an approach had no place in Lalor's vision because, as he wrote, "To the past we can never return, even if we would".[113]

Chartism and the Irish

As this survey of eighteenth-century radical writings has demonstrated, Lalor was by no means the first to challenge the fundamental rights of property in land. However, apart from Thomas Spence, none of those thinkers whose principles and doctrines have been examined proposed any form of public control over the land. Insofar as Irish nationalist opinion considered the land question at all it was in the context of Paine's writings, which in turn reflected the French Revolution's protection of individual property rights. In Ireland at

---

[110] Jim Smyth, *The Men of No Property: Irish Radicals and Popular Politics in the Late Eighteenth Century* (Basingstoke, 1998), pp. 167-8.
[111] *The Union Doctrine, or poor man's catechism* (c. 1796), as quoted in Smyth, *Men of No Property*, pp. 167-8.
[112] Ibid., p. 168.
[113] *Nation*, 24 Apr. 1847. (Ramón, *JFL*, p. 64.)

any rate, the dominance of Paine's ideas undoubtedly made it difficult for more radical thinking, such as Spence's plan, to compete. As mentioned above, even in his own country, Spence was a marginal figure. There, as Chase has argued in his study of English radical agrarianism, Spence's posthumous influence depended far more on personal connections made by his followers than in the dissemination of his writings.[114] Nevertheless, that influence persisted within the next notable manifestation of English radicalism: the Chartist movement.

Breaking the connection between landowning and political power was a central goal of Chartism from its inception. As detailed in the People's Charter published in 1838, the movement's founders wanted to expand the popular franchise and bring to an end the system "where property, however, unjustly acquired, is possessed of rights, that knowledge the most extensive, and conduct the most exemplary, fail to attain…"[115] Opposition to the status quo, whereby the land was owned by a small elite, pervaded Chartism. Indeed, as Chase has demonstrated, the very legitimacy of property rights in land was a longstanding issue for many Chartists, particularly when it came to the enclosure of the commons.[116] Although Chartism was essentially an English phenomenon, Irish-born immigrants made up a significant proportion of the membership and of the leadership. O'Higgins has argued that, given their predominately agrarian background, the Irish exerted a disproportionate influence on Chartist thinking about the land question.[117] Three examples illustrate this, even if they also demonstrate that there was no consensus among them as to the best means of reform.

Thomas Ainge Devyr

Thomas Ainge Devyr (1805-1887) was a radical journalist who became a leading Chartist and land reformer during the late-1830s. Born in Donegal, he moved to England in 1836.[118] Shortly before his departure, he published a pamphlet

---

[114] Malcolm Chase, *The People's Farm: English Radical Agrarianism, 1775-1840* (Oxford, 1988), p. 19.

[115] Workingmen's Association, *The People's Charter; being the outline of an act to provide for the just representation of the people of Great Britain in the Commons House of Parliament* (London, 1838), pp. 11-2.

[116] Malcolm Chase, "Chartism and the land: 'The mighty People's Question'", in Matthew Cragoe and Paul Readman (eds.), *The Land Question in Britain, 1750-1950* (Basingstoke, 2010), pp. 59-62.

[117] Rachel O'Higgins, "The Irish influence in the Chartist Movement", *Past & Present*, /20, Nov. 1961, p. 93.

[118] Michael J. Turner, *Radicalism and Reputation: the Career of Bronterre O'Brien* (East Lansing, MI, 2017), p. 169.

outlining his proposals to rectify what he saw as the root cause of Ireland's ills: "*absolute* ownership of land".[119] In his pamphlet, he appealed to Irish landlords to reduce rents and offer perpetual leases to their tenants. In effect, he was advocating the extension of the Ulster Custom to the rest of the country, much as Lalor was to do (under duress) at Holy Cross a decade later.[120] In recommending this solution to the Irish land question, Devyr was following in the footsteps of William Sharman Crawford, who campaigned repeatedly at Westminster for the Ulster Custom to be codified in law.[121] To underline his affiliation to Crawford's cause, Devyr dedicated his pamphlet to the Irish MP. Devyr continued his campaign for land reform in England, before emigrating again in 1840, this time to the United States. There, two years later, he republished his pamphlet.[122] He spent the remainder of his life in America agitating for and writing about the iniquities of the landholding system, both in Ireland and his adopted home.[123] During his short spell as a Chartist, Devyr was associated with two of the movement's most prominent leaders—each in his own way a leading advocate of land reform.

Feargus O'Connor

Feargus O'Connor (1796?–1855) was a nephew of Arthur O'Connor, whose preference for small farms over large estates is discussed above. Feargus was born in Cork and moved to England in the mid-1830s where he helped to establish the Chartists as a political force.[124] In 1845 O'Connor sought to give practical effect to his uncle's thinking by setting up the Chartist Co-operative Land Society. Its objective was "to settle families on the land as peasant smallholders".[125] O'Connor believed that factory workers and tenant farmers should learn to be self-sufficient in the production of their "daily bread", and break their dependence on both the "few owners of all [the country's] aggregate wealth", and on foreign food producers. By subscribing to the Land Society, they would become self-reliant because "our land, and that alone, is a branch of the national wealth with which no foreign state

---

[119] Thomas Ainge Devyr, *Our Natural Rights: a pamphlet for the people* (Belfast, 1836), p. vi.
[120] Ibid., pp. 33-5.
[121] James Quinn, "Crawford, William Sharman", *DIB* (Cambridge, 2009), (http://dib.cambridge.org/viewReadPage.do?articleId=a2168) 19 Feb. 2018.
[122] Devyr, *Our Natural Rights* (Williamsburg, 1842).
[123] Jamie L. Bronstein, *Land Reform and Working-class Experience in Britain and the United States, 1800-1862* (Stanford, Calif., 1999), pp. 123-4, 244.
[124] Maura Cronin, "O'Connor, Fergus (Feargus)", *DIB* (Cambridge, 2009), (http://dib.cambridge.org/viewReadPage.do?articleId=a6589) 17 Feb. 2018.
[125] G.D.H. Cole and A.W. Filson (eds.), *British Working Class Movements: Select Documents, 1789-1875* (London, 1951), pp. 398-401.

can by possibility interfere".[126] O'Connor's goal was a nation of small proprietors who, through owning their plots of land, would have a stake in their country's welfare.[127] While Devyr and O'Connor were most likely familiar with Spencean land policy, neither of their proposals endorsed the principle of communal landownership.[128] On the contrary, they are founded on the assumption that individual property rights would continue to be upheld. However, that assumption was not universal within the movement. Spence's more radical, and less popular, ideas found their natural heir in the form of the second of Devyr's erstwhile Chartist associates, James 'Bronterre' O'Brien (1804-1864).

James 'Bronterre' O'Brien

O'Brien was born in Granard, Co. Longford, and, like Devyr, was an almost exact contemporary of James Fintan Lalor. Shortly after his graduation in 1829 from Trinity College Dublin, O'Brien moved permanently to England where he quickly found his niche as a journalist in the radical press. There he made common cause with O'Connor and both men worked together in the early days of Chartism, most notably through O'Connor's newspaper, the *Northern Star*, to which O'Brien was a regular contributor.[129] During the 1830s and 1840s, O'Brien wrote articles on various topics, including land reform, for this and other newspapers and journals, many of which he published and edited himself.[130] By 1835 O'Brien had absorbed the writings of Ogilvie, Spence and Paine and was calling for "the appropriation of the whole soil of the country to the whole people of the country".[131] In the same article, he projected that, with the state as "sole landlord", annual revenues of "30 millions or more" could be generated "for national purposes".[132] To demonstrate that he had not forgotten his homeland, O'Brien spelt out his theory in relation to Ireland:

---

[126] Feargus O'Connor, *A Practical Work on the Management of Small Farms*, 4th edn (Manchester, 1846), p. 5.

[127] Joy MacAskill, "The Chartist Land Plan", in Asa Briggs, ed., *Chartist Studies* (London, 1959), pp. 305-6.

[128] In his autobiography published in 1882, Devyr challenged Spence's principle of common ownership of the land although he did not say when he first encountered it. See Devyr, *The Odd Book of the Nineteenth Century* (New York, 1882), p. 19.

[129] Fergus A. D'Arcy, "O'Brien, James ('Bronterre')", *DIB* (Cambridge, 2009), (http://dib.cambridge.org/viewReadPage.do?articleId=a6474) 17 Feb. 2018.

[130] Ibid.

[131] Alfred Plummer, *Bronterre: a Political Biography of Bronterre O'Brien, 1804-1864* (London, 1971), p. 180.

[132] *Poor Man's Guardian*, 28 Mar. 1835.

> [The Irish] require that the fee-simple of the land shall revert to the rightful owner, viz. The Nation, from which it never could be alienated without the general consent expressed by a majority—that the nation shall therefore resume its proper position as grand landlord of the whole country, and receive the rents henceforward in behalf of the people, to be divided share and share alike among every inhabitant, rich and poor, after defraying the expenses of government.[133]

As is clear from this extract, O'Brien's position was much more extreme than any of the British or Irish reformers discussed above—excepting Spence of course. Indeed, Barry has contended that O'Brien was responsible for the "earliest demand for true nationalisation of the land".[134] O'Brien continued to develop and refine his stance within Chartism and this brought him into conflict with O'Connor, whose land plan he opposed.[135] More significantly, his almost perfect prefiguring of Lalor's ideas was written 13 years before the launch of *The Irish Felon*. Moreover, O'Brien shared Lalor's antipathy towards Daniel O'Connell. In the same article, he lambasted O'Connell's failure to fight for "bread and justice" on behalf of the Irish.[136] Given these similarities, if Chartist writings on the land question helped shape the formation of Lalor's theories, it would not be surprising if O'Brien, rather than Devyr or O'Connor, turned out to be his chief influence. Is there any indication that such an influence existed?

While there is no direct evidence that Lalor ever came across any of O'Brien's writings on land nationalisation, there was, theoretically at least, an opportunity for him to have done so during his absence from Tinakill between 1844 and 1846. A few months after Lalor moved first to Dublin and then to Belfast, O'Brien relocated his press operation to Douglas in the Isle of Man in order to avoid British newspaper taxes.[137] In November of that year, he launched a weekly newspaper, *The National Reformer*, producing 75 editions before it ceased publication in April 1846. Significantly perhaps, the short life of O'Brien's newspaper coincided almost exactly with Lalor's period away from his father's controlling presence. Patt Lalor was a prominent supporter of Daniel O'Connell, who campaigned, largely successfully, to prevent the spread of Chartism into Ireland. It is unlikely, therefore, that Lalor senior would have undermined his

---

[133] Ibid., 13 Jun. 1835.
[134] Barry, *Nationalisation in British Politics*, p. 31.
[135] Turner, *Radicalism and Reputation*, p. 92.
[136] *Poor Man's Guardian*, 13 Jun. 1835.
[137] Michael J. Turner, "Ireland and Irishness in the political thought of Bronterre O'Brien", *IHS*, 39/153, May 2014, p. 52.

leader by allowing any Chartist journal into his home.[138] On the other hand, during his sojourns in the two largest cities in Ireland, his estranged son was free to read any of the many newspapers and journals on sale there.[139] However, whether or not *The National Reformer* was one of them cannot be readily ascertained. Unfortunately, because no trace of the first series of O'Brien's Manx newspaper venture has survived, details of its content and circulation are unknown.[140] Consequently, its relevance as a potential influence on Lalor's thinking about land tenure cannot be gauged with any certainty. Nevertheless, some informed speculation is appropriate if the brief history of O'Brien's next press endeavour is examined.

In October 1846, O'Brien relaunched his failed newspaper under the extended title of *The National Reformer and Manx Weekly Review of Home and Foreign Affairs*.[141] O'Brien was keen to assure his loyal readers that this was essentially the same newspaper as before. He designated the first edition as "No. 76. No. 1—New Series", in order to emphasise the link between the two organs. In the opening article he explained his strategy thus, "When, in April last, I was obliged to discontinue the *National Reformer*, I pledged myself to resume it the moment I got a favourable opportunity..." Reviving his paper would enable O'Brien as editor "to force our views and principles upon public attention in the best manner we can".[142] Like its predecessor the relaunched newspaper had a short life, ceasing publication in May 1847.[143] As the dates indicate, the second series of O'Brien's Isle of Man-based periodical was circulating after Lalor's return to Tinakill, where his access to the anti-O'Connellite press was heavily restricted. However, if both series of *The National Reformer* reflected the same editorial focus and values, then in its first incarnation O'Brien's newspaper may have contained much to stimulate Lalor's mind, had he read it.

After the potato blight struck Ireland in 1845 O'Brien took a keen interest in its effects. In each edition of his relaunched newspaper, he devoted a section to "Irish Affairs", drawing his reporting of the Famine from his reading of the Irish

---

[138] O'Higgins, "Irish Influence", pp. 86-7.
[139] It has been estimated that over a dozen newspapers were published in Dublin alone during the mid-1840s. (see Patrick Francis Tally, "The growth of the Dublin weekly press and the development of Irish nationalism, 1810–1879" (PhD thesis, University of Wisconsin-Madison, 2003), p. 106.)
[140] John Belchem, "The neglected "unstamped": the Manx pauper press of the 1840s", *Albion: A Quarterly Journal Concerned with British Studies*, 24/4 (1992), p. 614.
[141] Turner, *Radicalism and Reputation*, pp. 274-5.
[142] *National Reformer*, 3 Oct. 1846.
[143] Turner, *Radicalism and Reputation*, pp. 274-5.

press, including *The Nation*. He also covered political events in his home country, notably the secession of the Young Ireland group from O'Connell's Repeal Association, a move he welcomed "with rapture".[144] O'Brien repeatedly articulated his preference for land nationalisation as the most just form of land tenure, because it would benefit urban dwellers as well as rural tillers of the soil.[145] So here were the substantial themes of Lalor's writings being addressed in a manner that was largely in tune with his own views. If Lalor encountered similar content in the first series of O'Brien's paper, it may well have been a factor in the radical direction he took following his return to Tinakill. However, such a possibility must be treated with scepticism.

In each edition of his relaunched paper, O'Brien claimed that it "circulates in every county in England and Scotland, and in most of the Welsh and Irish counties..."[146] However, there is little evidence that it made much, if any, impression in O'Brien's home country. Subscriber details published each week reveal an overwhelmingly English and Scottish readership, with only a handful of addresses located in Dublin or Belfast.[147] Perhaps more tellingly, advertising was drawn exclusively from British or Manx sources. In 1843 O'Brien had accused Irish newsagents of boycotting his previous periodical, *The Poor Man's Guardian and Repealer's Friend*, perhaps at O'Connell's instigation.[148] A similar response may explain *The National Reformer's* lack of success in Ireland. Even away from his father's disapproving oversight, therefore, it seems that the chances of Lalor finding O'Brien's newspaper in either city were slim. Nevertheless, he may well have been aware of O'Brien's activities as a Chartist leader and a journalist through occasional reports in the Irish press.[149] Furthermore, Lalor seems to have become sympathetic to Chartism as his own published writings grew more radical. As described in the next chapter, his articles in *The Irish Felon* reached Chartists sympathetic to O'Brien's thinking on land. Lalor himself appealed through *The Irish Felon* for an "English Chartist of known talent and honesty" to help run the paper.[150] However, despite the obvious alignment between the political and social perspectives of both men, a clear thread of influence cannot be discerned. At a deeper level, this should not be surprising.

---

[144] *National Reformer*, 7 Nov. 1846
[145] Ibid., 5 Dec. 1846.
[146] Ibid., 17 Oct. 1846.
[147] Ibid., 3 Oct. 1846, 10 Oct. 1846.
[148] Turner, "Ireland and Irishness", p. 51.
[149] *Freeman's Journal*, 20 Mar. 1839. *Nation*, 27 May 1843.
[150] *Irish Felon*, 8 Jul. 1848 (Ramón, *JFL*, p. 129.)

Notwithstanding the similarity of their common Irish background, their ideas on land tenure, a shared aversion to Daniel O'Connell, and their involvement in radical journalism, the relative outlooks of O'Brien and Lalor were very different. O'Brien's translation of Buonarroti's *History of Babeuf's Conspiracy for Equality* and his influential role in the life of George Julian Harney, an associate of Marx and Engels, placed him squarely at the heart of an international radical tradition that stretched from the extreme wing of the French Revolution to the development of communism a half-century later.[151] While O'Brien retained a keen interest in his native land, he was not a separatist like Lalor. O'Brien supported a more limited form of local legislature than was advocated by Young Ireland in the belief that, under a single imperial parliament in London, ties between Britain and Ireland would be strengthened.[152] His radical orientation derived less from a devotion to Irish nationalism as much as from a concern about class inequalities.[153] Lalor's interest in land reform, on the other hand, was bound up in his intense nationalism. As demonstrated in the previous chapter, he was at heart a conservative farmer, radicalised by the unprecedented catastrophe that followed the potato blight, and which was exacerbated, in his eyes, by a grossly unjust system of land tenure imposed on Ireland by Britain.

Despite these fundamental differences, it is difficult to argue against the judgement of the Chartist leader's most recent biographer that "O'Brien might have had a better understanding of Irish politics had he reflected more deeply upon such a resource as Lalor's journalism".[154] However, it would be wrong to infer from this that O'Brien was not familiar with Lalor's published writings. Shortly after the original appeared in *The Nation*, O'Brien published an extract from Lalor's second article under the headline, "A true account of the Irish famine and its consequences". In his introduction to the piece, O'Brien praised Lalor's analysis of landlord/tenant relations as "the best exposition we have yet seen of the true state of Ireland, as it is, and as the landlords design it to be—a vast Golgotha, or charnel-house."[155]

Perhaps, if *The National Reformer* had continued its run into the summer of 1848, O'Brien might have realised that his views on land nationalisation were shared by his fellow Irishman. However, his brief mention of Lalor appeared in that paper's final edition. O'Brien returned to the British mainland shortly

---

[151] Neil Harding, "Marx, Engels and the Manifesto: working class, party, and proletariat", *Journal of Political Ideologies*, 3/1 (1998), p. 33.
[152] *National Reformer*, 5 Dec. 1846.
[153] Turner, *Radicalism and Reputation*, p. 250.
[154] Ibid.
[155] *National Reformer*, 29 May 1847.

afterwards and spent much of the following year embroiled in Chartist infighting. In November 1848, he launched his next publication, *The Power of the Pence*, but he had apparently missed the full expression of Lalor's thinking on the land question in *The Irish Felon* and the prospect of any alliance between the two reformers was lost.[156] In any event, radical land reform was just one element of the sophisticated doctrine that Lalor conceived, and that doctrine in its completed form was unique to him. Nonetheless, another Irish writer had already considered a possible link between nationalism and landholding, and this was a figure whom Lalor knew of and admired.

Thomas Davis

In his second letter to the Confederation leaders in January 1847, Lalor articulated the thoughts of many when he wrote, "Oh, for one year of Davis now!'[157] He was referring to the Young Ireland leader and regular contributor to *The Nation*, Thomas Davis (1814-1845), who had died little more than a year earlier. As he set forth on his own literary journey, Lalor clearly felt the loss of a man whose "voice would have now been louder than mine, to say what mine is too feeble to say".[158] Davis was *de facto* co-editor of *The Nation* and its chief editorial writer, so Lalor would have been familiar with his writings since the paper's launch in 1842.[159] Davis' articles reflected his love of Irish culture and history, which for him were the hallmarks of the distinct nation to which he aspired.[160] He also displayed a keen interest in the land question and his *Nation* articles on the subject must have impressed Lalor. For instance, in an early editorial headlined "Aristocracy—The result of conquest", Davis attacked the parasitic nature of the Irish landowning class which had so weakened the people that they "have been laid helpless at their feet". He called on those same people to oppose this unwanted domination, not with "unmeaning murders" and "partial insurrections", but by call[ing] with one voice for a complete remodelling of the laws affecting landed property".[161] How those laws might be remodelled led Davis to research the land systems in operation in other countries.

Prior to the launch of *The Nation* Davis wrote a series of articles on the history of India, focusing in particular on its conquest by Britain.[162] Drawing upon Sir

---

[156] Turner, *Radicalism and Reputation*, pp. 83-5.
[157] *Irish Felon*, 1 Jul. 1848. (Ramón, *JFL*, p. 126.)
[158] Ibid.
[159] Andrews, *Newspapers and Newsmakers*, pp. 19-20.
[160] Quinn, *Young Ireland*, p. 16.
[161] *Nation*, 3 Dec. 1842.
[162] Quinn, *Young Ireland*, p. 35.

John Malcolm's memoirs of his time serving as a British diplomat in India, Davis highlighted the security of land tenure enjoyed by the peasants in that country.[163] Every one of them, according to Davis, "had a tenant-right to the land he cultivated". In effect, this meant that "The soil belonged to the farmer, not to the noble, and this right was never questioned".[164] As Quinn has argued, in examining the political and social conditions in other conquered nations, Davis hoped to expand the perspective of Irish nationalists who might otherwise imagine that their country's situation was somehow unique.[165] So he extrapolated from his reading of Malcolm to declare a universal truth that he clearly believed applied as much to Ireland as to India:

> The land of a nation is the property of the nation, or property and nation are but terms in a tyrannous riddle, without justifiable or intelligible meaning. Where the soil comes, by usage or long usurpation, to be considered the property of the rich or noble, the people must of necessity be enslaved; and enslaved they must remain, while such tenures continue to subsist.[166]

Despite his apparent identification of land ownership with national sovereignty, Davis did not infer any kind of communal land ownership from his Indian research. What appealed to him about the Indian land system was the security of tenure that prevailed there. In other words, smallholders paid rent to landlords as they did in Ireland, but they were not subject to arbitrary eviction.[167] However, as he continued to explore the customs and laws in other countries during the early-1840s, Davis's views on land tenure became more nuanced.

In 1842 the *Dublin Monthly Magazine* published a lengthy article by Davis in which the author offered another alternative to the Irish situation, this time originating in Norway.[168] Presenting the country as having been until recently "the half-savage province of Sweden", Davis identified a small nation which, like Ireland, had endured the predations of its neighbour from time to time. More to the point, Davis had learnt from his reading that Norway had managed to keep its

---

[163] Robert Eric Frykenberg, "Malcolm, Sir John (1769–1833), diplomatist and administrator in India." *ODNB*, [http://ezproxy-prd.bodleian.ox.ac.uk:2167/view/10.1093/ref:odnb/9780198614128.001.0001/odnb-9780198614128-e-17864] 6 Mar. 2019.
[164] Thomas Davis, "India - her own and another's", *Dublin Monthly Magazine, being a new series of The Citizen*, 1/4, Feb. 1840, p. 262.
[165] Quinn, *Young Ireland*, p. 35.
[166] Davis, "India", p. 262.
[167] Ibid.
[168] Thomas Davis, "Udalism and Feudalism, I & II", *Dublin Monthly Magazine*, Mar/Apr. 1842, pp. 218-37, 293-315.

ancient form of land tenure more or less intact, i.e. Udalism.[169] Like Ireland, Norway's economy was, Davis asserted, predominately based on agriculture. Yet, as he put it, "the Irish peasant is a rack-rented tenant; the Norwegian peasant is a free proprietor, the absolute lord of his little farm."[170] This situation obtained, Davis' desk research told him, because the Norwegian land was not subject to any superior claim by crown or noble.[171] However, the relatives of an individual landholder retained a stake in his property, such that it was difficult for him to sell it to an outsider without consulting them. Thus, a kind of tribal or clan-based tenure in the land co-existed with the individual's property rights.[172] According to Davis, the result of this system was that, compared with their Irish counterparts, Norwegian rural dwellers enjoyed a superior quality of life in terms of food, clothing and shelter.[173] Davis' examination of the Norwegian land system seemed to be leading him towards a more radical position than the mere extension of tenant right suggested by the Indian example. As he concluded in the article's final paragraphs, "Make the mass of landholders proprietors instead of dependants, and the aristocracy will crumble in the presence of the people".[174] Yet, if Davis now favoured peasant proprietorship, he also acknowledged that Ireland's historical landholding system had a communal dimension at odds with the contemporary notion of individual and absolute property rights. In the first part of his article, Davis contrasted the form of tribal tenure that obtained in pre-Norman Ireland with the system of regal lordship imposed by England during the seventeenth century. The former, in Davis' analysis, corresponded closely to the Udal law of Norway, in that family or kin rights over land came into force when the landholder died.[175] The English system, on the other hand, had, he contended, ensnared Ireland in a plethora of primitive feudal laws that had long outlived their usefulness in every other European country, including Britain itself.[176]

As is clear from this brief analysis, Davis never went as far as Spence, O'Brien, and Lalor in elevating the community's rights above those of the individual landholder. That is not to suggest that his investigations into the tenure systems in India and Norway had no bearing on the development by Lalor of his own theories. When Lalor was trying to forge links, first with the Peel government

---

[169] Ibid., pp. 218, 225.
[170] Ibid., pp. 295-7.
[171] Davis' source on Norway was Samuel Laing, *Journal of a Residence in Norway, during the years of 1834, 5, and 6* (1 vol. 8vo. London, 1836).
[172] Davis, "Udalism and Feudalism", p. 297.
[173] Ibid., pp. 299-310.
[174] Ibid., p. 314.
[175] Ibid., pp. 219-24.
[176] Ibid., p. 225.

and then with the Irish landowners, Davis had already concluded that the fundamental problem underpinning the Irish land question was the stranglehold in which the peasants were gripped by "an alien aristocracy, who have the administration of justice, local taxation and expenditure, and a control over the representation in their hands".[177] Therefore reforming the Irish land system was, for Davis, the first priority because it is "a question of life or death with the people".[178] Yet he also urged caution. He declared, long before Lalor did, that the landlords would "never yield to [the] demand… for udal tenures" as long as they were "supported by a foreign army".[179] So notwithstanding his references to the appalling conditions of the Irish peasantry, even in those pre-Famine times, Davis was already considering the merit of combining the hitherto distinct goals of better land tenures and national self-determination, a strategy which he deemed not to be "unwise". His thinking may have been half-formed, and his expression tentative and couched in rather ungainly prose, but Davis at least hinted at the central tenet of Lalor's later doctrine when he concluded his survey of Norwegian land tenures with this striking comment:

> Some may think, that agitated alone, the demand for proprietorship would end in some paltry and unprincipled compromise, but that if kept as an ulterior result of nationality, and agitated as one of its blessings, it will be won by the same effort…[180]

Davis urged his readers to debate this "solemn subject…in fairs and markets, in church and by the fire-side, in festivity and business…"[181] Although, as argued above, Lalor probably never encountered the radical views of Spence or O'Brien, it is quite possible that his admiration for Davis' writings in *The Nation* brought the earlier pieces discussed above to his notice. If so, Davis' tentative link between land and nationalism may have sparked the idea in Lalor's mind that led him to his famous railway engine simile.[182] That, of course, is speculation but, given the gaps in the primary sources, the task of tracing the genesis of Lalor's policies on land tenure is necessarily speculative.

Somewhat less hypothetical, however, is the possibility of continental influence. References to France and the French Revolution in the Lalor archive, and in his

---

[177] Ibid., p. 314.
[178] Ibid., p. 315.
[179] Ibid.
[180] Ibid.
[181] Ibid.
[182] It must be remembered that Lalor envisaged land as the "engine" that would carry independence with it. Davis, on the other hand, seems to have seen settlement of the land question as a consequence of the national question being resolved.

published writings, indicate another factor to be considered in tracing the origins of his thinking.

A French connection?

As described in Chapter One, Fogarty claimed that Lalor visited France twice. She drew on oral history in support of her contention but cited no specific sources in either edition of her collections.[183] Although sceptical of Fogarty's claims, O'Neill also referred to the "oral tradition" of Lalor's supposed French sojourns, the first of which may have been in 1830 and the second in 1848.[184] This raises the intriguing prospect of Lalor having witnessed both the July Revolution of 1830 and the February Revolution of 1848, or at least their aftermaths. Kelly's objection that "No Letters or documents mention such an expedition" could be attributable to the gaps in the primary sources described in the previous chapter.[185] However, if Lalor had been to France, it is odd that Luby did not record some reference to it in his gossipy memoirs. Nonetheless, contrary to O'Neill's assertion, there is evidence that Lalor had some interest in and knowledge of the country and its culture.[186] For example, in one of his *Irish Felon* articles setting out his proposal for a joint-stock company to keep the newspaper going, he cited in support of his proposition the example of *Le Siècle*, a contemporary French daily newspaper.[187] Of itself, this does not prove that Lalor read the paper, either in France or in Ireland, because the Irish press regularly carried stories from *Le Siècle* during the 1840s.[188] However his awareness of the nature of that paper's proprietorship suggests an interest beyond that of the casual reader. That interest may be linked to the presence in the Tinakill library of several French-themed books.[189] These included a *Histoire de France* and Adolphe Thiers' *History of the French Revolution* ("part 1st only"), which was available in English translation as early as 1838.[190]

Whether or not Lalor read Thiers' book, his interest in the 1789 Revolution is clear from his first published article in *The Nation*. In it, he contrasted the degrading effects of the "revolution" in Irish society wrought by the Famine, with the positive effects of the French Revolution, which, Lalor asserted, "took

---

[183] Fogarty, *JFL*, p. xxii. Fogarty, *JFL* (1947), p. xvi.
[184] O'Neill, *JFL*, p. 27. Fogarty, *JFL*, p. xxviii.
[185] Fogarty, *JFL* (1997), pp. 2-3.
[186] O'Neill, *JFL*, p. 27.
[187] *Irish Felon*, 8 Jul. 1848. (Ramón, *JFL*, p. 128.)
[188] e.g. *Cork Examiner*, 14 Jun. 1848.
[189] NLI, Ms. 8570/02.
[190] M.A. Thiers, *The History of the French Revolution*, tr. Frederick Shoberl (5 vols, London, 1838).

France to the sun—gave her wealth, and victory, and renown—a free people and a firm peasantry, lords of their own land".[191] While Lalor's satisfaction with this outcome is apparent, it evidently did not go far enough for him. As is clear from a reading of "The Faith of a Felon", Lalor saw both the 1789 and 1848 revolutions as "unfinished business".[192] They had, he wrote, resulted in "The right of the people to make the laws". Another revolution was needed, however, to bring about "The right of the people to own the land". Such a goal would have been unnecessary if Lalor believed that post-revolutionary French property laws were sufficient to form the basis for the system of landholding he envisaged for Ireland.

1848 and the rise of Socialism

In "The Faith of a Felon" Lalor proposed that tenant farmers should withhold rents from their landlords as a first step in securing both national independence and sovereignty over the land. Once this was achieved, "those rents shall be paid to themselves, the people, for public purposes".[193] As discussed above, this was not a novel idea, having already been proposed by Spence and Bronterre O'Brien. However, Lalor's article appeared in the summer of 1848 when all of Europe was in revolutionary ferment. Ireland's burgeoning radical press offered numerous opportunities for the circulation of once marginal ideas, including the concept of rent as a form of national tax. During that fateful year, Lalor's was not the only voice advocating such a measure. Before examining the most famous of these other voices, two local examples are worth mentioning. These can be found in the pages of *The Irish Tribune*, a newspaper that produced only five editions before being closed down in July 1848.[194]

The second issue of the *Tribune* included the transcription of a paper read at a meeting of the Irish Polytechnic Institute entitled "On the tenure of land".[195] According to the report, the author cited biblical authority to argue that,

---

[191] *Nation*, 24 Apr. 1847. (Ramón, *JFL*, p. 63.)
[192] French National Assembly draft constitution: "Art. 115. The confiscation of property can never be re-established... [Art.] 127. All property of every description is inviolable." (*Irish Tribune*, 24 Jun. 1848).
[193] *Irish Felon*, 8 Jul. 1848 (Ramón, *JFL*, p. 134.)
[194] Patrick M. Geoghegan, James Quinn, "O'Doherty, Kevin Izod", *DIB* (Cambridge, 2009), (http://dib.cambridge.org/viewReadPage.do?articleId=a6680), 24 Feb. 2018.
[195] *Irish Tribune*, 17 Jun. 1848.

this earth was given as common property, not to privately enjoy the land, divide and subdivide it into private possessions, but to cultivate it, and enjoy the fruits of it.

The unknown author went on to propose how this principle could be applied to Ireland in a scheme that amounted to a limited form of land nationalisation. It would involve transferring to "the crown" all uncultivated lands in private ownership, plus church lands. These would then be leased out to smallholders in return for rent payments. The resulting revenues would be sufficient, claimed the author, "to defray all our taxes". This national income could be increased even more if "the aristocracy" also paid rent to the crown in respect of their remaining property. Two weeks later another anonymous contributor to the same newspaper went further in an article under the headline, "The land for the rightful owners".[196] The writer advocated seizure by the state of lands held by proprietors who refused to join "the popular movement". Such lands would then be granted, in lots of no more than 500 acres, "to those who may be approved of as having capital and skill to conduct such farm" (sic). The accumulated rent payments would constitute, the article proclaimed, "a yearly state tax, towards defraying all expenses". The rationale for such a measure, according to the article, was that "The ground… belongs to the people at large and not to a class…"

The concept of landholders paying rent to the state, rather than to landlords, was also included in Karl Marx's *Manifesto of the Communist Party*, first published in February 1848. In it, Marx admitted that his programme for centralised control by the state of "all instruments of production" would necessitate "despotic inroads on the rights of property". These "inroads" would include "[the] Abolition of property in land and application of all rents of land to public purposes".[197]

The similarity of these proposals to Lalor's proposition on rent in "The Faith of a Felon" is plain. Lalor's article appeared on 8 July, several weeks after the first of *The Irish Tribune* examples described above, and a week after the second. Both newspapers operated out of the same premises in Trinity Street, Dublin, so the possibility of a contributor to one, such as Lalor, seeing a preview of the rival paper cannot be ruled out.[198] However, this is a theoretical possibility only. Given that the impetus for "The Faith of a Felon" came from Duffy's piece in *The Nation* of 29 April, Lalor probably began to draft his response several weeks

---

[196] Ibid., 1 Jul. 1848.
[197] Karl Marx and Friedrich Engels, *The Communist Manifesto* (London, 1985), p. 104.
[198] John Mitchel, *The Last Conquest of Ireland (perhaps)* (Glasgow, 1882), pp. 193-5.

before it was published. Furthermore, it is evident from the content that Lalor's proposition on rent was the product of much thought and discussion with other people, and unlikely to have been a case of opportunistic plagiarism.[199] Indeed, he claimed that he had communicated his policy on rent to his Confederation correspondents more than a year before.[200]

In any event, the theory of rent as national income seems to have entered radical discourse quite quickly during 1848, its most notable appearance occurring in Marx's seminal publication. However, the *Manifesto* was written and printed in German and published in London and gained little attention at the time.[201] If copies somehow appeared in Ireland at the same time, they made no impact on the public consciousness. Therefore Lalor could not have known of its existence, let alone its content, when he wrote his article. It must be remembered that Lalor believed from the start, i.e. January 1847, that his teachings on land tenure would make Ireland "the lode star of history". It seems unlikely that, if he was merely purloining ideas already in circulation, he would have predicted in the same letter that his country would become "an original inventor" as a result of those same teachings. Perhaps a quotation from historian Marc Bloch can be said to apply in this case:

> With all due respect to the criticism of plagiarism, whose spirit denies the spontaneous repetition of events or words, coincidence is one of those freaks which cannot be eliminated from history.[202]

Whether Lalor's rent proposal arose from some external influence or his own untainted inspiration is not as important as the connection he made between it and Irish separation from Britain. If that twin-concept was devised in half-formed fashion by Thomas Davis, Lalor developed and perfected it. Yet, even Davis' influence on Lalor in this regard cannot be established with any degree of certainty. If Lalor himself is to be viewed as a reliable witness to his own evolution as a radical visionary, then his theories on the Irish land question arose not from the work of other thinkers, whether Irish or foreign, but from his critical analysis of the law governing land tenure.

Blackstone and Locke

The small library at Tinakill included the four volumes of the *Commentaries on the Laws of England* by William Blackstone (1723-1780). First published

---

[199] *Irish Felon*, 8 Jul. 1848. (Ramón, *JFL*, pp. 135-6.)
[200] Ibid., (Ramón, *JFL*, p. 133.)
[201] A.J.P. Taylor, "Introduction", in Marx, *Communist Manifesto*, pp. 7, 48.
[202] Marc Bloch, *The Historian's Craft*, (Manchester, 1992), p. 102.

between 1765 and 1769, the *Commentaries* exerted a profound influence on British and international legal practice throughout the nineteenth century.[203] Indeed the quotation on land tenure from *Encyclopaedia Britannica* at the beginning of Chapter One was taken verbatim from the *Commentaries*.[204] The only source material that Lalor explicitly referenced in his published writings was the second volume of Blackstone's magnum opus, which dealt with property rights.[205] In his opening chapter, Blackstone defined the primal relationship between the land and the people:

> The earth, therefore, and all things therein, are the general property of all mankind, exclusive of other beings, from the immediate gift of the creator.[206]

According to Blackstone, "the word 'land' included not only the face of the earth, but every thing under it, or over it", or as the Latin phrase states, *cujus est solum, ejus est usque ad coelum* ("who owns the soil, his it is even to heaven").[207] As has been detailed in Chapter One, Lalor embraced these principles and restated them often in his public and private writings, e.g. "up to the sun and down to the centre".[208] However, he freely altered many of Blackstone's other precepts—which he dismissed as having been "*invented by theorists*"—to suit his own ideas about land tenure.[209]

Blackstone made it clear that his definition of the earth as "the general property of all mankind" referred to a time when humans existed "in a state of primeval simplicity".[210] He argued that, as populations spread and society grew more complex, the concept of permanent and exclusive dominion over land became necessary, and so individual property rights took precedence over common ownership. Such rights, Blackstone asserted, arose from the fact of "occupancy", and were legitimised by the "implied assent" of the wider community.[211] He cited John Locke (1632-1704), who contended that "As much land as a man tills, plants, improves, cultivates, and can use the product of, so

---

[203] Wilfrid Prest, "Blackstone, Sir William (1723–1780)", *ODNB*, [http://ezproxy-prd.bodleian.ox.ac.uk:2167/view/article/2536] 20 July 2017.
[204] Blackstone, *Commentaries*, ii, p. 59.
[205] *Irish Felon*, 8 Jul. 1848 (Ramón, *JFL*, p. 137.)
[206] Blackstone, *Commentaries*, ii, p. 3.
[207] Ibid., ii, p. 18.
[208] NLI, Ms. 340/61.
[209] *Irish Felon*, 8 Jul. 1848 (Ramón, *JFL*, p. 137.)
[210] Blackstone, *Commentaries*, ii, p. 3.
[211] Ibid., pp. 4-9.

much is his property".[212] Blackstone interpreted this as making even "implied assent" unnecessary.[213] Lalor disagreed with this analysis, claiming that it could be used to justify the depredations of Attila the Hun—as well as the seizure of Irish land by Britain. Rejecting what he termed "this feeble and fictitious right of occupancy", Lalor insisted that Blackstone's "imperfect compact" of "implied assent" must give way to "a positive and precise grant from the people". The unacceptable alternative was the appropriation of the land by force, an outcome, he maintained, that could never be valid irrespective of the passage of time.[214] Rejecting both Blackstone and Locke, Lalor declared that exclusive property rights could apply only to what an individual had created himself, thereby excluding land from his definition.[215]

As O'Neill noted, Lalor took issue also with Blackstone's styling of the king as "lord paramount", whose rights over the land were not bound by "temporal limitations".[216] Blackstone underlined the royal prerogative by quoting the medieval maxim, *Nullum tempus occurrit regi* ("No time runs against the king"), or as a modern authority has interpreted it, "a sovereign is not bound by any temporal limitations…"[217] Lalor subverted this ancient doctrine, rendering it instead as "*Nullum tempus occurrit Deo — nullum tempus occurrit populo*".[218] In Lalor's new society, no king would intrude between God and the people. "[T]hey, and none but they," he wrote to Mitchel, "are the first landowners and lords paramount as well as the lawmakers of this island".[219] In his *Commentaries*, Blackstone drew upon the historical record in support of his interpretation of property rights. An important milestone in the development of "feudal tenures" in England, according to Blackstone, was King William's domesday-book. This established the system whereby the king's vassals submitted their lands to him in an act of "homage and fealty to his person".[220] As illustrated above, Lalor recast this medieval concept of allegiance in accordance with his vision of a new Ireland ruled by its people. On that basis,

---

[212] John Locke, *Two Treatises of Government*, 5th edn (London, 1728), p. 163.
[213] Blackstone, *Commentaries*, ii, p. 8.
[214] *Irish Felon*, 8 Jul. 1848 (Ramón, *JFL*, pp. 139-41.)
[215] Ibid. (Ramón, *JFL*, pp. 137-8.)
[216] O'Neill, *JFL*, p. 55.
[217] Blackstone, *Commentaries*, ii, p. 259. Aaron X. Fellmeth and Maurice Horwitz, "Nullum tempus occurrit regi" *Guide to Latin in International Law.* (Oxford, 2009). [http://www.oxfordreference.com/view/10.1093/acref/9780195369380.001.0001/acref-9780195369380-e-1499] 21 Jul. 2017.
[218] *Irish Felon*, 8 Jul. 1848 (Ramón, *JFL*, p. 141.)
[219] JFL to Mitchel, 21 Jun. 1847, RIA 12.P.15/7.
[220] Blackstone, *Commentaries*, ii, p. 49.

"Destitute of books"

land would be granted to loyal citizens just as it had been in feudal times. However, allegiance would be determined by the people themselves, or their representatives in a national assembly.

In rejecting Blackstone's theory of first occupancy, Lalor dismissed also the philosophers and conceptualists whose writings on landed property formed much of the source material for the *Commentaries*, or as he succinctly put it, "Messrs. BLACKSTONE, TITIUS, LOCKE and Co."[221] There is no evidence that Lalor ever read Locke or any of the other sources cited by Blackstone, e.g. Grotius, Pufendorf or Jean Barbeyrac (1674-1744).[222] Nonetheless, as a devoted if somewhat frustrated bibliophile, he certainly knew of Locke's work if only through his reading of Blackstone. If "Blackstone's second book" was "the only page I ever read on the subject [of the rights of property in land]", it suggests that Lalor's long interest in the Irish land question was not fuelled by extensive reading of publications such as those discussed in this chapter.[223] That would hardly be surprising given both the paucity of printed material available to him in Tinakill, and the late development of his radical outlook. It does, however, mark him out from the other land reformers described above, all of whom drew inspiration from earlier writings on the subject of land tenure, whether philosophical or political in tone. Locke's *Second Treatise*, in particular, is an oft-cited source, irrespective of the writer's position on individual versus communal property rights. Many of the writers discussed above appropriated and adapted Locke's ideas on land to suit their own agendas.[224]

***

The problem in seeking to identify influences on the development of any subject's thinking has been analysed meticulously by Skinner in a notable paper.[225] In the case of Lalor, Skinner's observation that it is virtually impossible to exclude coincidence or randomness before attributing influence to an earlier thinker is hard to refute.[226] Yet, while Lalor's breakthrough idea to link the land and national questions may have been his own invention, all the elements he

---

[221] *Irish Felon*, 8 Jul. 1848 (Ramón, *JFL*, p. 137.)
[222] The name "Titius" was used in legal texts as a hypothetical everyman when discussing examples of case law. Its inclusion in Lalor's list of "theorists" may have been intended as irony, or it may reflect his ignorance of the legal and philosophical sources used by Blackstone.
[223] *Irish Felon*, 8 Jul. 1848 (Ramón, *JFL*, p. 137.)
[224] Chase, *The People's Farm*, p. 143. (see also Ogilvie, *Right of Property in Land*, pp. 15, 188. Spence, *Rights of Man*, pp. 23-4.)
[225] Quentin Skinner, "Meaning and understanding in the history of ideas", *History and Theory*, 8/1 (1969), pp. 26-7.
[226] Ibid.

used to construct his theory existed already. In Britain, the encroachment by landowners on previously commonly-used spaces precipitated new thinking on the rights of the individual versus the community. While some participants in this discussion accepted, however reluctantly, the system of exclusive property rights that had evolved over centuries, others sought to overturn it. Radical theorists, such as Spence and O'Brien, wished to transfer ownership of all land from the individual to the community, whether that was represented by the parish or the state. That they anticipated Lalor's very similar ideas by several decades is beyond question. What remains unresolved, however, is whether or not any of their writings influenced him. More easily settled is the extent to which Lalor was inspired by the Young Ireland writings in *The Nation* and elsewhere. He clearly shared the romantic, and sometimes mystical, concept of Ireland and its history which he probably absorbed through the works of Davis, Mangan, etc.

As his use of the "queen-metaphor" demonstrates, Lalor entered into areas of thought that would have been foreign to Spence, and even to his fellow Irishman, Bronterre O'Brien. The conclusions he arrived at indicated a singular breadth of vision that embraced both the political and the philosophical. On the one hand, he championed separation over repeal, a political objective that left him closer to the United Irishmen than the Young Irelanders, but which was also within the bounds of contemporary comprehension. On the other hand, he envisaged Ireland, not as a piece of real estate to be owned outright by a handful of wealthy individuals, but as a living presence to be served and protected by all the people. Such a concept, it seems, was beyond common understanding. When Lalor's ideas were first circulated among the Irish Confederation council members, it is hardly surprising that, according to D'Arcy McGee, they "spread in silence".[227]

As an auto-didact with very little exposure to formal education, Lalor missed out on the opportunities to learn about, and debate with others, great ideas and discoveries. These were opportunities that his contemporaries, Duffy, Davis, Mitchel, etc., were able to avail of at institutions like Trinity College, Dublin. Lalor's access to books was limited and, given his exceptional intellect, this was a source of constant frustration. Yet his relative isolation may have brought some benefits. He was free to explore questions of legal theory and political economy without the intellectual constraints that exposure to early-nineteenth-century academic teaching might have imposed. So when the blight and subsequent famine began to devastate the people, he could bring together disparate aspects of his learning, without any concern as to whether or not they conformed to the received wisdom of his time. Thus he was able to

---

[227] McGee to JFL, 20 Mar. 1847, NLI, Ms. 340/103.

grasp much more quickly than anyone else both the threat and opportunity presented by the Famine. Consequently if any factor can be said to have been the central influence on Lalor's theory of land tenure and national sovereignty it is the Famine. That cataclysmic event transformed a conservative, middle class farmer's son into a radical thinker. As referenced in Chapter One, the principles and theories he espoused found a receptive audience among Irish nationalists and reformers in the late-nineteenth and twentieth centuries. The reception of his ideas by Lalor's contemporaries was a different matter, however, and is the subject of the next chapter.

CHAPTER THREE

"I SOMETIMES WISH FOR SOME ONE TO SPEAK TO": LALOR AND HIS CONTEMPORARIES

The brevity of Lalor's journalistic career, coupled with the general instability caused by famine and revolution, militated against a reasoned discussion of his ideas by his contemporaries. Adding to these unsettling factors was the lack of clarity and consistency which sometimes characterised his public utterances on land tenure and repeal. Yet, as indicated in the previous chapters, he made a considerable impact, whether among the leaders of the Irish Confederation, at the gathering at Holy Cross, or in the editorial office of *The Times*. In this chapter, a systematic analysis of the response to Lalor's ideas by his contemporaries will be undertaken. The analysis will include those family members, friends, associates, and members of the public whose reactions have been recorded, whether during Lalor's own lifetime or in memoirs written after his death.

Lalor's peers

Among those of Lalor's contemporaries who were concerned about the Irish land question, three in particular are worthy of discussion.

John Marnell

The archive includes about two dozen letters sent to Lalor by his friend, John Marnell. Little is known about Marnell, other than that he was a farmer living in Wicklow who shared his friend's interest in land reform.[1] The cache of letters spans a two-year period, beginning in April 1846—nine months before Lalor's first contact with *The Nation*—and ending in May 1848—just prior to the appearance of the *Irish Felon* articles. Unfortunately these documents represent only half the correspondence as Lalor's letters are presumed to be lost. Nevertheless, because Marnell sometimes recapitulated points from his friend's letters in his replies, it is possible to gain some insight into the other side of the exchanges. For example the political differences between the two men are evident from Marnell's observation that, "You are not a repealer. Why you are not so I do not understand".[2] In relation to the land question, Lalor may

---

[1] O'Neill, *JFL*, p. 34.
[2] Marnell to JFL, 6 Nov. 1846, NLI, Ms. 340/119

have used the correspondence to test and rehearse his ideas before revealing them to a wider audience. By early 1847, just after he had initiated contact with the Confederation, Lalor's views on land tenure were raising some disquiet in Marnell's mind. In a striking phrase, Marnell alluded to "your peculiar views on the tenure question". In the same letter Marnell offered his own tentative summary of his friend's position: "You are convinced that the people of Ireland are the rightful owners of Ireland—of its land as well as of its law—I do not know whether I understand you".[3] If Marnell had difficulty in grasping the full extent of his friend's thinking, subsequent letters from Lalor provided a little more insight, if not much grounds for agreement between the two friends. For instance Marnell responded to a challenge to the landowners' right of ownership made by Lalor.[4] It would seem that Lalor was contesting the legitimacy of the right of occupancy secured through the English conquest of Ireland. Marnell's reply makes it clear that, while he agreed that the landlords had acquired their property "by might at least, if not by right", he accepted the status quo and believed it to be pointless to try to reverse or overturn the facts of history. Just before the publication of Lalor's first article in *The Nation*, Marnell tried to sum up their respective positions:

> Meanwhile, let us endeavour to understand one another. We are agreed that the tenantry are entitled to the use of the land on a secure tenure and on conditions, one of which is to be the payment of a fixed and fair money rent. You ask, "But under whom and from whom should they hold their lands, etc., etc." You have my opinions—from the landlords with the state as umpire and protector between them. I must rather infer yours. Will you be good enough to state in full what are your opinions, what your principles…[5]

It seems that after a year-long correspondence, Marnell could not quite comprehend how far his friend's stance on the land question diverged from his own more conventional understanding. If Lalor ever did respond to Marnell's request for clarity, it is not referred to or reflected in the remainder of the correspondence. Nor is it known what Marnell made of Lalor's *Irish Felon* articles as the extant correspondence ends two months before they were published.

Even if he was unaware of the similarity between his ideas on land tenure and those of Spence and O'Brien, Lalor understood how radical they were in the context of 1840s Ireland. He believed, however, that they should be considered carefully by nationalist leaders in light of the calamitous state of the country. As

---

[3] Marnell to JFL, 8 Feb. 1847, NLI, Ms. 340/125.
[4] Marnell to JFL, 29 Mar. 1847, NLI, Ms. 340/128.
[5] Marnell to JFL, 5 Apr. 1847, NLI, Ms. 340/129.

argued in Chapter One, Lalor had already reached a firm conclusion on the questions of repeal and landholding by the time he approached the Young Irelanders. Perhaps the Marnell correspondence taught Lalor to be cautious about detailing the full radical nature of his thinking for fear of alienating those who might become his allies. As described in Chapter One, Lalor often held back from a candid and comprehensive exposition of his views after he entered the public sphere. For example, he went along with the Confederation policy of courting the landlords, even though he believed that the prospect of them ever supporting repeal was a "forlorn hope".[6] At Holy Cross, he dropped his call for a rent strike under pressure from Doheny. Even when he gained greater control over his published writings at *The Irish Felon*, he felt constrained by the need to maintain the support of his associates. When the *Felon's* editor, John Martin, went on the run following the police raid on the newspaper's premises, Lalor wrote to the "Under-Secretary for Ireland" stating that the articles and letters which appeared under his name "were published in opposition to [Martin's] expressed opinion".[7] As outlined in Chapter One, those writings, while more frank than anything Lalor had previously allowed into the public domain, were not wholly explicit about his principles of landholding and property rights. If Martin was reluctant to publish Lalor's ideas even in qualified form, "The Faith of a Felon" might never have appeared in the newspaper under his editorship.[8] As it happened, Lalor's most famous article was printed in the third issue of *The Irish Felon*. Tellingly, this edition was produced during Martin's absence as he tried to evade arrest.[9]

William Conner

Although little is known about the early years of Lalor's engagement with the land question, he was, prior to his entry onto the public stage, an associate of a well-known land reformer, William Conner (d. 1852).[10] Conner was an

---

[6] *Irish Felon*, 1 Jul. 1848. (Ramón, *JFL*, p. 121.)

[7] *Irish Felon*, 8 Jul. 1848.

[8] Corroboration for Lalor's statement to the Under-Secretary can be found in Martin's letter to John Mitchel dated 6 Apr. 1848: "We want no disturbance of the settlement of property in Ireland, or of social order, except what is just, and what may be necessary for the existence of our people, as freemen, by their own industry." (see P. A. Sillard, *The Life and Letters of John Martin, with sketches of Thomas Devin Reilly, Fathers John Kenyon, and other "Young Irelanders"* (Dublin, 1893), p. 69.

[9] *Irish Felon*, 8 Jul. 1848.

[10] Little information about William Conner's personal life has survived and his birth and death dates are unknown. (see Patrick Maume, "Conner, William", *DIB* (Cambridge, 2009), (http://dib.cambridge.org/viewReadPage.do?articleId=a1950) 4 May 2018)

illegitimate son of the United Irishman, Arthur O'Connor, and a first cousin of Chartist leader, Feargus O'Connor, both discussed in the previous chapter.[11] Conner began his public career as a land reformer in 1832 with a speech delivered at Inch in Queen's County, a little over 10 miles from Tinakill.[12] In it he proposed a remedy for what he described as the "all-devouring rack-rent" imposed on tenant farmers by the "idle or property class":

> ...the legislature should interpose on your behalf by passing a Bill for an applotment or valuation of land, by which all lands already let, or hereafter to be let, shall be brought down to their fair value...[13]

Conner's valuation would be based on "the raw uncultivated soil" and made "by a sworn jury of men".[14] Because the produce of the tenant's "skill, industry, and capital" would be excluded from the valuation, his rent would fall—in Conner's estimation by as much as 30%.[15] In 1835 Conner published a pamphlet combining his original speech with a new introduction. This incorporated an additional legislative measure, suggested to Conner by James MacGrady and the aforementioned John Marnell, to provide perpetuity of tenure to the tenant as long as he paid his rent.[16]

During the years that followed, these two elements, fair valuation and perpetuity of tenure, became the hallmark of Conner's doctrine, which he propounded frequently through his speeches and writings.[17] By March 1843, such was his reputation that Daniel O'Connell himself proposed Conner, "a gentleman of great talents, personal activity and zeal", as a member of the Loyal National Repeal Association.[18] In his address to the association in June, O'Connell set out the objectives and policies of the association under such headings as self-government, church-state relations, and the land question. As described in Chapter One, O'Connell proposed a land policy based on the principle of tenant right, as advocated by Sharman Crawford.[19] In preparing for his address, O'Connell considered Conner's alternative plan of valuation and perpetuity. While he regarded that plan, as "a most benevolent one", he

---

[11] George O'Brien, "William Conner", *Studies*, 12/46, Jun. 1923, p. 279.
[12] William Conner, *The Speech of William Conner against Rack-Rents* (Dublin, 1832).
[13] Ibid., p. 5.
[14] Ibid., p. 14.
[15] Ibid., p. 15.
[16] William Conner, *The True Political Economy of Ireland* (Dublin, 1835). O'Neill, "Irish Land Question", p. 328.
[17] e.g. William Conner, *The Axe Laid to the Root of Irish Oppression* (Dublin, 1840).
[18] *Nation*, 4 Mar. 1843.
[19] Ibid., 10 Jun. 1843.

rejected it partly because it was likely to inspire opposition from the landlords, who, in his view, "ought not to be treated so harshly".[20] This setback does not seem to have affected Conner's standing within the association. In September he chaired one of the weekly meetings when O'Connell was away.[21] However, Conner's favoured status was not to last. During the leader's continuing absence Conner moved that, until such time as both repeal and his own preferred land reforms were in place, the Association should support a rent-strike.[22] The members were outraged that Conner would "propound doctrines that were wholly inconsistent with the principles…that O'Connell always inculcated…", i.e. a rent-strike.[23] Before he could be expelled, Conner tendered his resignation.[24] At the next meeting of the association, O'Connell "declared him to be the enemy of the people of Ireland", and ordered "that the name of William Conner be expunged from [the association's] books".[25]

Following Conner's failed attempt to force his policy of valuation and perpetuity back on the Repeal Association's agenda, he continued his one-man campaign to reform the land laws. Four years later, in September 1847, he turned up at the Holy Cross meeting of tenant farmers described in Chapter One. Just after Lalor's final resolutions had been carried, Conner ascended the platform and began to address the assembly. When he was some minutes into a lengthy speech on the iniquities of the present landlord-tenant system, Lalor intervened to try to regain control of the agenda. An unseemly brawl ensued bringing the meeting to a premature end. Before that abrupt conclusion, Lalor and Conner engaged in a heated argument. Their exchanges were included in the press accounts of the meeting which appeared shortly afterwards.[26] These reports revealed that Lalor and Conner had once been allies in the cause of land reform, but that Lalor had severed the connection when Conner was expelled from the Repeal Association for what Lalor termed as "a dangerous and discreditable resolution".[27] Lalor's stance at Holy Cross, which followed the Confederation line of opposition to a rent strike, thereby seems to have fostered an impression in Conner's mind that he was the more radical of the two, prompting his charge at Holy Cross that "my

---

[20] Ibid., 15 Apr. 1843.
[21] *Leinster Express*, 16 Sep. 1843.
[22] *Nenagh Guardian*, 20 Sep. 1843.
[23] *Nation*, 23 Sep. 1843.
[24] Ibid.
[25] Ibid., 30 Sep. 1843.
[26] *Freeman's Journal*, 20 Sep. 1847. *Nenagh Guardian*, 22 Sep. 1847. *Tipperary Vindicator*, 22 Sep. 1847.
[27] *Tipperary Vindicator*, 22 Sep. 1847.

principles so shock him now".²⁸ Yet, just before his unscheduled appearance, Lalor had moved two resolutions that encapsulated Connor's core principles of valuation and perpetuity. As demonstrated in Chapter Two, even these measures represented a compromise on Lalor's part. His articles in *The Irish Felon* illustrated how much his thinking had altered since his association with Conner, and revealed his true position on land tenure to be much more radical than that of his old colleague. Indeed, like most of the reformers discussed in Chapter Two, Conner supported the rights of private property in land and favoured the continuation of the landlord/tenant relationship, albeit in an arrangement that prevented exorbitant rent increases or capricious evictions.²⁹ On the national question, Conner differed markedly from Lalor. During his brief time in O'Connell's Repeal Association, Conner assured the members that he was "not, as to government, a republican", and that he believed Ireland should remain subject to Britain and to "our loved Victoria".³⁰

O'Neill maintained that Lalor was "intimately associated with William Conner since about 1831".³¹ In the preface to his edition of Fogarty's collection, Kelly speculated that "Lalor almost certainly attended [Conner's first meeting in 1832], since it took place at Inch, not far from his home".³² If true, this indicates that Lalor's relationship with Connor lasted more than a decade, and that his interest in the land question may have been sparked by his initial contact with Conner.³³ That Lalor broke the connection because of Conner's support of a rent-strike underlines the former's conservative stance at the time. Yet, only a few years later, Conner was the conservative in comparison to his erstwhile associate's views on land and nationalism. Nevertheless, it is plain even from the sparse evidence available that Conner exerted a significant influence on Lalor. That influence was twofold. Firstly, the relationship must have deepened Lalor's knowledge of the Irish land system as he accompanied the older reformer on his peregrinations around the country. More specifically, it seems likely that he drew upon Conner's theories for the Holy Cross resolutions relating to tenant right and the impartial rent tribunal. Indeed it may have been his failure to acknowledge Conner as the source of these measures that provoked the latter's intervention. Although Lalor went on to advocate a form of nationalisation of Ireland's land, with the rent paid to the state rather than to private landlords, Conner's concept of independent

---

[28] Ibid.
[29] William Conner, *A Letter to the Tenantry of Ireland: containing an exposition of the rackrent system* (Dublin, 1850), pp. 11-17.
[30] *Nation*, 19 Aug. 1843.
[31] O'Neill, "Irish Land Question", p. 332.
[32] Fogarty, *JFL* (1997), pp. 4-5.
[33] NLI, Ms. 340/59.

valuation would have been a prerequisite for such a system to find public acceptance. It must be concluded, therefore, that without Conner's influence, Lalor might not have developed his interest and knowledge of the land question when he did.

As for Conner, he continued to expound his principles unchanged. In a pamphlet published in 1850, he combined the familiar arguments for valuation and perpetuity with fierce criticism of his rivals. Although he did not mention Lalor by name, his rather bitter reference to "the deception of the ephemeral crowds who have of late become your pretended advocates... writers for newspapers and other periodicals..." may have reflected his painful experience at Holy Cross.[34] If Conner ever read or heard about his former associate's *Irish Felon* articles, they or their author do not appear to have made any impact on him during the remaining years of his solo crusade.

William Sharman Crawford

There is no evidence that Lalor ever met another prominent land reformer of the day, William Sharman Crawford (1780–1861). Crawford was a landowner and landlord from County Down who permitted the Ulster Custom to be practised by his tenants.[35] As a member of the British parliament between 1835 and 1852, he introduced numerous bills to legalise tenant right throughout Ireland. However, none managed to achieve majority support.[36] Lalor was aware of Crawford's espousal of tenant right and mentioned the Ulster reformer in his correspondence with John Marnell. Lalor's new radical perspective led him to castigate Crawford, Conner, and Marnell himself, for not enlisting the support of "an active and energetic party—an army of talent, a powerful Journal", as he was about to do.[37] Crawford was aware of Lalor's efforts during 1847 to organise the farmers of Tipperary, and unsurprisingly did not approve. In a letter to a rival tenant league in the same county, written just before the Holy Cross meeting, he denounced gatherings "which would create the apprehension of danger to the just rights of property".[38] In a follow-up letter

---

[34] Conner, *Letter to the Tenantry of Ireland*, pp. 23-4.
[35] William Sharman Crawford, "Sharman Crawford on Ulster Tenant Right, 1846", ed. Brian A. Kennedy, *IHS*, 13/51, Mar. 1963, pp. 246-53.
[36] James Quinn, "Crawford, William Sharman", *DIB* (Cambridge, 2009). (http://dib.cambridge.org/viewReadPage.do?articleId=a2168) 10 Jul. 2017.
[37] Marnell to JFL, 5 Apr. 1847, NLI, Ms. 340/129.
[38] *Tipperary Vindicator*, 2 Oct. 1847.

sent shortly after the Tipperary assembly, he expressed satisfaction to his correspondent that "you are not connected with Mr. Lalor's meeting".[39]

The Lalors of Tinakill

Lalor was guarded in the expression of his ideas because he learnt to expect little understanding or encouragement from others. This was true even among his immediate family members. Although Lalor was the first-born of a very large family, his relationships with his parents and 11 siblings were not uniformly close. Almost inevitably during that era, he lost some close relatives through emigration or death. For instance, his brother Jerome left Ireland in March 1845 when James Fintan was living in Dublin.[40] His mother died in 1835, as did his brother Joseph.[41] Although not naturally an introvert, Lalor seems to have grown accustomed to being alone. Perhaps this was at least partly due to the disability that marked him out as different from others. During one of his lengthy absences from Tinakill, he wrote that:

> I lead almost as solitary a life as that of Saint Simon Stylites, without any of the motives and feelings which sustained and enabled him to enjoy or endure it. Nobody I think, can bear solitude better than I can; yet I sometimes wish for some one to speak to.[42]

This was written following the row with his father and his departure from Tinakill in 1844. Whatever may have been behind the dispute, it seems to have been brewing for some time. In May 1843, when four of his brothers appeared with their father at a repeal rally in Queen's County, James Fintan was absent.[43] However, while the basis of these interpersonal difficulties is unclear, they seem to have run deeper than mere political differences over O'Connell and the repeal movement.[44] A student of the Lalor family has asserted that the poor relations between them "emanated from Patt Lalor's endeavours to manipulate his children's lives".[45] As is demonstrated below, James Fintan was not the only

---

[39] Ibid.
[40] Jerome Lalor to JFL, 8 Mar. 1845, NLI, Ms. 340/88.
[41] O'Neill, *JFL*, p. 9.
[42] JFL to RL, 12 Apr. 1845, NLI, Ms. 8563/9.
[43] *Freeman's Journal*, 31 May 1843
[44] The extent of the rift can be judged from a letter to Patt Lalor from James Fintan, sent following his departure from Tinakill: "your conduct... deeply injured and wronged, if not ruined me, beyond remedy or reparation, both in this world and the next..." (see JFL to PL, 7 Aug. 1845, NLI, Ms. 8563/11).
[45] Michael G. O'Brien, "The Lalors of Tenakill 1767-1893" (M.A. thesis, St. Patrick's College, Maynooth, 1987), p. 77.

one of Lalor senior's children to resent their father's controlling tendency. In the eldest son's case, it seems to have led to permanent estrangement. An insight into the relationship can be found in Luby's memoirs of his time travelling with James Fintan in 1849, only months before the latter's death. He recorded Lalor as remarking that, "My father's house, Luby, is still open to me any time I choose to accept his terms."[46] Whatever the cause, the surviving letters in the Lalor archive testify to the fractious nature of the relationship between father and eldest son. However, they reveal little about Patt Lalor's attitude to James Fintan's renewed preoccupation with the land question following his return to Tinakill in early 1846. If the Lalors ever discussed the younger man's thinking about nationhood and land tenure, those exchanges are lost to history. Yet, on the latter question at least, father and son shared a sense of dissatisfaction with the status quo.

Patrick ('Patt') Lalor: paterfamilias and reformer

Like his son in the late-1840s, Patrick ('Patt') Lalor was prepared to consider radical solutions in addressing a perceived injustice, as he did when he took a leading role in the Tithe War of the 1830s. A tithe was an ancient tax designed to support the established Church. From the sixteenth century, the imposition of tithes required the majority Catholic population of Ireland to pay for the upkeep of a religious institution whose doctrines and rituals they largely shunned.[47] Opposition to the tithe system took violent form in the eighteenth and early nineteenth centuries through the activities of secret societies such as the Whiteboys and the Ribbonmen.[48] In 1830 a concerted campaign by farmers against the payment of tithes began in County Kilkenny and spread from there.[49] Patt Lalor led the resistance movement in Queen's County, achieving such prominence that in December 1832 he was elected to the British House of Commons as an MP.[50] Earlier that same year he was among those who gave evidence before a select committee established by the British parliament to investigate the non-payment of tithes.[51] When he was asked to suggest how the present impasse might be overcome, Lalor senior proposed that church lands

---

[46] *Irish Nation*, 11 Mar. 1882.
[47] D. J. Hickey and J. E. Doherty, *A Dictionary of Irish History* (Dublin, 1987), pp. 561-2.
[48] Gale E. Christianson, "Secret societies and agrarian violence in Ireland, 1790-1840", *Agricultural History*, 46/3, July 1972, pp. 374-5.
[49] Patrick O'Donoghue, "Causes of the opposition to tithes, 1830-38", *Studia Hibernica*, /5, 1965, pp. 8-9.
[50] Hourican, "Lalor, Patrick ('Patt')".
[51] *The Times*, 16 Dec, 1831.

should be nationalised and let to tenants. The rent received would then be used to pay the clergy, with any surplus allocated to other purposes. If the rents were insufficient to replace the tithe payments to Protestant clergy, Lalor suggested that the additional burden should be placed on landowners via a property tax.[52] The radical nature of Patt Lalor's proposal could not have been lost on the committee, whose members were surely aware that, less than half-a-century earlier, Church lands in France were seized by the revolutionary government.

Following the Tithe War Lalor senior maintained a keen interest in the land question and in 1844 he gave evidence before the Devon Commission when its members visited Abbeyleix. When asked how landlord/tenant relations could be improved, Patt Lalor proposed that tenants should be granted permanent tenure as long as they paid their rent to the landlord. The agreed level of rent would be reviewed every few years in line with the average price of a staple crop, such as wheat.[53] His plan, he reassured his interlocutors, would not "injure the landlord", rather it would grant him "an increased rent, an increased security".[54] In a striking passage in his written testimony, Lalor reminded the commissioners of the constraints on ownership of property in land:

> Before any landlord or tenant had any individual interest (except as members of the state) in the land it belonged to the state. The state transferred certain rights in the land, but not an unrestricted or unlimited ownership; it transferred it subject to the support of the state in the shape of taxation, subject to have any of it re-occupied by the state which may be found necessary, and above all, it was transferred saddled with the support of the population.[55]

Lalor senior's analysis is effectively an elaboration of Thomas Drummond's assertion made in 1838 to Tipperary landowners that "Property has its duties as well as its rights".[56] This was an inconvenient reminder of the theoretical concept of landholding articulated by Blackstone (See Chapter One), but largely forgotten by those landholders who clung to their individual property rights. Patt Lalor's statement also foreshadowed the famous principle enunciated by his son at Holy Cross and in his newspaper articles:

---

[52] *Parliamentary Papers* (1831-32), 508, XXI.245, Second report from the select committee of the House of Commons on tithes in Ireland, p. 379.
[53] Ibid., p. 334.
[54] Ibid.
[55] Ibid., p. 607.
[56] O'Brien, *Thomas Drummond*, p. 284.

> I hold and maintain that the entire soil of a country belongs of right to the people of that country, and is the rightful property not of any one class, but of the nation at large, in full effective possession, to let to whom they will on whatever tenures, terms, rents, services, and conditions they will... [57]

Both men seem to have shared a common understanding of the uniquely communal dimension that underpinned landholding. Whereas James Fintan believed it could be restored in the new Ireland he envisaged, for his father it meant simply, as he put it in his submission, that "people have not an unlimited or unrestricted right to do what they like with their own"..."[58] So when Patt Lalor called for "a substantial and radical change in the law and practice between landlord and tenant", he was not questioning the practical rights of private property in land.[59] Although by no means as "radical" as the proposals made by Spence and O'Brien, Patt Lalor's plan to overhaul the land laws was similar to those presented by Ogilvie, Paine, and the other likeminded reformers discussed in Chapter Two. They accepted that the existing system of landholding need not be overturned in order to make it more equitable. Like them, Lalor senior did not question what his eldest son later referred to as "the robber's right by which the lands of this country are now held in fee for the British crown".[60] Yet he showed himself willing to challenge the widespread assumption among the landowning class in Ireland that the rights of their tenants were inferior to their own. It must be remembered also that he made his stand before a panel of landlords, and long before his son entered the public arena. Perhaps, in their respective analyses of the land question, little separated the two men—if they could have put aside their personal differences. This was the view of James MacGrady who, in a long letter to *The Tipperary Vindicator* in the wake of the Holy Cross meeting, described Patt Lalor as his "valued friend". He urged father and son to "[act] together in promoting the cause of the tenantry of Ireland, instead of acting separately".[61] If anything, however, the onset of the potato blight only deepened the division between the two men.

While the famine and the subsequent British response drove the younger Lalor to contemplate a "revolution which will leave [Ireland] without landlords", his father continued to promote reform within the current system. Almost three years after he appeared before the Devon Commission, Lalor

---

[57] *Irish Felon*, 24 Jun. 1848 (Ramón, *JFL*, pp. 103-4.)
[58] *Parl. Paps.* (1845), Cm 657, XXI.1, p. 607.
[59] Ibid., pp. 607-9.
[60] *Irish Felon*, 24 Jun. 1848 (Ramón, *JFL*, p. 107.)
[61] *Tipperary Vindicator*, 29 Sep. 1847

senior reiterated his evidence in a letter to *The Tipperary Vindicator*, still convinced that his proposal to improve tenant security was superior to "all other plans that I have seen..."[62] In April 1849, while his son plotted rebellion, Patt Lalor wrote to Sharman Crawford, seeking his support in parliament for improved rights for tenant farmers.[63] Meanwhile, through his political and personal connections in Queen's County and beyond, Lalor senior must have been aware of his son's increasingly public activism. Fogarty alleged that Daniel O'Connell himself sympathised with Lalor senior at the "[loss of] support of his eldest son".[64] It seems that, given his prominent position in the Repeal Association, the older man was embarrassed by James Fintan's opposition to that body's aims.

In September 1847, at a banquet held in Kilkenny to honour a pro-repeal landlord, Charles Hely, Patt Lalor brought the differences between himself and his son to public attention. In a widely reported speech, Lalor senior criticised the forthcoming meeting at Holy Cross.

> He begged to state that he was not cognizant of that proceeding, and he deeply regretted the step which his son had taken, because he looked upon his plan as wild and visionary (hear).[65]

Patt Lalor's remarks were prompted by a newspaper report, in which a transcript of a printed "handbill" being circulated by "James F. Lalor" to publicise the Holy Cross event was quoted.[66] It announced that a "League of Tenant-Farmers" would be established in Tipperary to "settle... for ever... the question between Landlord and Tenant". In its commentary on this development, the paper adopted a surprisingly measured tone. So while the writer urged the organisers to adhere to Crawford's moderate agenda, he did not seem especially troubled about the possible boycotting of the payment of rent and rates, "highly as we respect the rights of property". It is likely, therefore, that Patt Lalor's use of the term "wild and visionary" was intended as a judgement on the overall direction being taken by his son. In any event the widely-reported Kilkenny dinner presented an ideal opportunity for a loyal O'Connellite to condemn extremism, even when it emanated from within his

---

[62] Ibid., 21 Jul. 1847
[63] PL to Crawford, 24 Apr. 1849, NLI, Ms. 8562-3/9.
[64] Fogarty, *JFL*, p. xviii.
[65] *Freeman's Journal*, 18 Sep. 1847. See also *Tipperary Vindicator*, 22 Sep. 1847 and *Leinster Express*, 25 Sep. 1847.
[66] *Dublin Evening Post*, 11 Sep. 1847.

own family. His remarks drew a warm response from the Repeal Association's new leader, John O'Connell, who told his members that,

> I myself heard [that excellent man, Mr. Patrick Lalor] declare at Kilkenny, that [the Holy Cross demonstration] was an ill-advised proceeding; and the report of that meeting, which appears in today's newspaper, shows that Mr. Lalor was not mistaken.[67]

The report of the Kilkenny gathering contains the only extant record of Patt Lalor's attitude to his son's proposals on land reform. If their differences ruled out any prospect of an alliance between them on the national or land questions, James Fintan found support elsewhere in the family through his younger brother, Richard (1823-1893).

Richard Lalor: brother and reluctant ally

Although the archive contains correspondence between James Fintan and several of his surviving siblings, most of the extant family letters are between him and Richard.[68] James Fintan's letters, especially those written in 1845 during his absence from Tinakill, suggest a particularly close relationship between the two brothers.[69] It seems that James Fintan relied on Richard to send him much-needed funds from time to time, as well as copies of *The Nation*.[70] After James Fintan entered public life early in 1847, he spent long periods away from Queen's County. He relied on his brother for news about local developments, as well as for financial support. Richard shared his brother's brand of assertive nationalism and, like James Fintan, he took the Young Ireland side following the split with the O'Connellites. However, unlike his older brother, he would not risk being ostracised by their father. In a letter explaining why he did not attend the Holy Cross gathering, Richard revealed that Patt Lalor had threatened him with "expulsion from Tinakill" were he to join his brother at the Tipperary meeting. Richard defended his decision to stay at home:

> I would sacrifice a great deal for the public, but this certainly I would not. And if I were to do so it would only be the means of leaving me powerless, both for the present and future, of doing any good.[71]

---

[67] *Leinster Express*, 25 Sep. 1847.
[68] The survival of so much correspondence between the two brothers is probably due to Richard having inherited the family farm on his father's death in 1856.
[69] See, for example, JFL to RL, 12 Apr. 1845, NLI, Ms. 8563/9.
[70] JFL to RL, 25 Jun. 1845, NLI, Ms. 8563/10.
[71] RL to JFL, 25 Oct. 1847, NLI, Ms. 340/94.

Clearly Richard was not going to follow his brother into exile and penury, but he would provide whatever assistance he could, "as long as I can without letting [my father] know".[72] Richard was anxious to persuade his brother that it was economic necessity rather than cowardice that stopped him defying their father openly. "[I]f I had any mode of living in the world besides what I have", he wrote, "I would not suffer twenty hours under such restraint".[73] By the summer of 1848, James Fintan's irritation at his younger brother's continuing fear of parental disapproval was growing. He wrote demanding that Richard travel to Dublin, "even if father be dying".[74] However Richard's half-hearted support for his older brother's activities was not due solely to his father's opposition. He had reservations, not only about the views James Fintan was expressing in his newspaper articles, but about his strategy of using the press to bring about social and political change: "The class you write for never read and the class that reads are only frightened by your writings".[75] Whether Richard was referring to his brother's opinions on revolution or landholding is unclear.

None of the extant correspondence contains any reference by either man to the questions of property rights or land tenure. Following Patt Lalor's death in 1856, Richard inherited both the family farm and his father's status as a nationalist leader in Queen's County.[76] At a public gathering in 1868, he was hailed as "Patt Lalor's son, the man who did away with the tithes".[77] Unsurprisingly it was his father's rather than his brother's ideas about land reform that he reiterated in public. Just as Lalor senior had argued before the Devon Commission that tenants should enjoy the security of tenure as long as they paid a fair rent, so too did Richard a quarter-century later in an open letter to the new British prime minister, William Gladstone.[78] In line with his father's position, Richard also assured his local MP, Kenelm Thomas Digby, that he would not "deprive [our present landlords] of one penny of their present income which they are justly entitled to".[79] Although he had once aligned himself with his brother's pursuit of social and political revolution, Richard was not a radical at heart. He followed his father into the British House of Commons and became a Home Ruler and a

---

[72] RL to JFL, 30 Oct. 1847, NLI, Ms. 340/96.
[73] Ibid.
[74] JFL to RL, 17 Jul. 1848, NLI, Ms. 8563/5.
[75] RL to JFL, 12 Jul. 1848, NLI, Ms. 340/97.
[76] Hourican, "Lalor, Patrick ('Patt')".
[77] *Leinster Express*, 21 Nov. 1868.
[78] Ibid., 20 Nov. 1869
[79] *Nation*, 12 Dec. 1868.

Parnellite.[80] He associated with Isaac Butt and Michael Davitt and continued to promote tenant right through the period of the Land War.

Young Ireland

As has been indicated in the previous chapters, James Fintan Lalor's principles and proposals received a mixed reaction from the Young Irelanders. Some were more willing than others to embrace the radical direction in which he sought to lead them.

Charles Gavan Duffy

Charles Gavan Duffy tried to harness Lalor's powerful prose in support of the Confederation's goal of creating a broad pro-repeal alliance that included landlords. However, after Holy Cross, Lalor's brand of nationalism became too extreme for moderates like Duffy. When the two men met as inmates in Newgate Prison in the latter part of 1848, Duffy tried unsuccessfully to dissuade Lalor from embarking on another insurrection after the failure of the recent rebellion in Tipperary.[81] A half-century later, Duffy described his one-time associate as "a thoroughly honest and remarkably able man, but", he recalled, "our paths distinctly separated". That separation occurred because Duffy came to believe in constitutional politics as the best means of achieving the aims of Irish nationalism.[82] On the question of land tenure and property rights, there is no record of any exchanges or arguments between the two men. Duffy made only one brief reference to Lalor's theories several decades afterwards:

> Mr. Lalor has been erroneously quoted as an advocate for the proposal known as the "Nationalisation of Land" (a proposal to make land the permanent property of the State), but it will be seen that his intention was widely different.[83]

Duffy's comment was probably made in response to the commentary surrounding George's *Progress and Poverty*. If Duffy never engaged directly with Lalor on the land issue, their differing positions on that topic, as well as on the broader national question, are evident from a reading of both "The Creed of 'The Nation'" and "The Faith of a Felon". Nevertheless, although Duffy did not accept Lalor's radical theories of landholding, he does seem to have absorbed a little of their essence.

---

[80] Fogarty, *JFL*, p. 140.
[81] Duffy, *My Life in Two Hemispheres*, i, pp. 314-7.
[82] Ibid., i, p. 316.
[83] Duffy, *Four Years of Irish History*, p. 480 (fn).

Several months after his release from prison in April 1849, Duffy relaunched *The Nation* with a new editorial policy. In his first leader since the paper was closed down more than a year earlier, he rejected even the limited repeal objective that had been a central demand of the Irish Confederation. In the first of two articles, headlined "The New "Nation", Duffy proclaimed his revised policy:

> Ireland is a sick and disabled man who we must strengthen and invigorate with many preliminary successes before he is able to win his last and most precious right.[84]

The enormous changes that had taken place in Ireland during *The Nation's* absence compelled Duffy to re-evaluate old assumptions. Many of his fellow Young Irelanders, Mitchel, Doheny, McGee, etc. had been driven into foreign exile in the wake of the 1848 rebellion. He had seen for himself the devastation caused to rural communities by the Famine, whether through starvation, disease, or emigration.[85] Yet, like Lalor a few years earlier, Duffy saw the possibility of a new society emerging from the wreckage. Echoing sentiments expressed by his former associate, Duffy wrote in the second part of his new manifesto, "A Famine like a Revolution heralds an era of sudden changes, and new beginnings".[86] The terrible catastrophes afflicting Ireland represented, he declared, the "tumultuous and prolific agony that precedes a new birth".[87] However, the immediate fruit of that painful process would not be any form of national self-determination:

> Independence is no longer the first achievement, and sole spring-head of all that will enrich and ennoble our country, but the end result of many previous victories.[88]

Whereas Lalor had linked the twin goals of independence and land reform, Duffy now decoupled them. Self-government was no longer the primary goal. Instead, Duffy proposed a national effort "beginning with that which is fundamental—that on which we all, directly or remotely, rest—the Land".[89] He elaborated in the second part of his article:

---

[84] *Nation*, 1 Sep. 1849.
[85] Ibid.
[86] Ibid., 8 Sep. 1849.
[87] Ibid.
[88] Ibid., 1 Sep. 1849.
[89] Ibid.

> I think the Land question is to be got settled first, and forthwith. It cannot wait for an Irish Parliament.[90]

If Duffy's renewed focus on the land question was influenced by Lalor, his strategy was much more moderate. Duffy offered a vivid metaphor of both the problem and his preferred solution:

> A mountain lies in our path, and I cannot pretend we will leap over it. Our road lies round the base and no other way.[91]

In other words, there would be no rent strikes, no peasant insurrections, and no wholesale ejection of landlords. Instead, Duffy proposed a process of "committees, lectures, conferences, deputations, reports".[92] He envisaged "a national association" and a "Parliamentary Party" working together "to help ourselves", and doing so while Ireland remained within the United Kingdom.[93]

In the following months, Duffy set about forming a broad coalition of interests to advance his plan. By May 1850 a committee had been formed and it announced that a national conference was to be held in Dublin.[94] In August, the inaugural meeting of Duffy's new national Tenant League was held. Gathered around him were some of the men who had opposed Lalor's plan a few years earlier, e.g. Patt Lalor and William Conner. Parliamentary business prevented Duffy's first choice as chairman, Sharman Crawford, from attending.[95] In contrast to the meeting at Holy Cross, most speakers were clergymen, Catholic or Presbyterian. The Rev Dr Kearney, PP, Kilkenny West emphasised the new body's peaceful and constitutional strategy and promised that it did "not contemplate the slightest infringement on the just rights of the landlords". Nevertheless, some of Duffy's new associates aspired to significant reform. The third resolution sought not only legalisation of the Ulster Custom throughout the country, but "the regulation of rent by a just and impartial valuation".[96] Although these steps did not go as far as the radical programme outlined two years previously in *The Irish Felon* by James Fintan Lalor, they corresponded with the measures agreed at Holy Cross. Indeed it could be argued that Lalor's compromise agenda in 1847 became the *de facto* blueprint for Duffy's enterprise three years later. For

---

[90] Ibid., 8 Sep. 1849.
[91] Ibid.
[92] Ibid.
[93] Ibid.
[94] Charles Gavan Duffy, *The League of North And South. An Episode in Irish history, 1850-1854* (London, 1886), pp. 36-7.
[95] Ibid, p. 52.
[96] *Freeman's Journal*, 10 Aug. 1850.

example, Lalor's inclusion of a resolution advocating a "fairly constituted and impartial tribunal" was a direct antecedent of the motion approved by Duffy's Tenant League. However, despite the similarities, the League's programme garnered a more positive response than had Lalor's ill-fated initiative.

Central to establishment endorsement were the expressions of support for property rights expressed at the conference. The pledge to uphold "this great and fundamental principle" won the approval of *The Freeman's Journal*, and its leader writer assured the paper's readers that the "social fabric" would not be disturbed by the resolutions passed at the event.[97] At the weekly meeting of the Loyal National Repeal Association, its leader John O'Connell devoted most of his address to a somewhat rambling, self-contradictory, but largely positive response to what he termed "a most blessed sight". While he voiced some reservations about the "silly or ridiculous yet dangerous expressions" he had seen in reports of the conference, there was nothing in the substance of the proceedings that "every honest and Christian man throughout the three kingdoms" could object to.[98] Despite much popular support for the new Tenant League it failed to fulfil its promise, largely due to disputes between the principal organisers.[99] Eventually, in despair at the collapse of the dream which had occupied him for the previous five years, Duffy decided to quit both his job and his homeland. In his last editorial for *The Nation*, Duffy announced his retirement from Irish public life and his intention to move himself and his family to Australia.[100]

Duffy's land plan may have enjoyed as little immediate success as Lalor's. However, Duffy lived long enough to see the passing of Gladstone's Land Law (Ireland) Act, 1881, which copper-fastened in law the practice of the Ulster Custom, previously legalised in 1870. In addition, one of the act's main provisions was a tenant's right to apply to the Land Court to have his rent fixed, if he received a demand for an increase.[101] Not surprisingly, Duffy complained that neither Gladstone nor the Land League leaders had "acknowledge[d] where the principles of the Land Act of 1881 were first successfully formulated and made articles of popular belief".[102] While there is merit in Duffy's charge, he did not himself

---

[97] Ibid., 12 Aug. 1850.
[98] Ibid., 13 Aug. 1850. O'Connell's support was shortlived. He subsequently rejected the proposal to regulate rates by valuation as "a ridiculous impossibility". (see Duffy, *League of North and South*, p. 63.)
[99] Terence Dooley, "Land and the people", in Alvin Jackson (ed.), *Oxford Handbook of Modern Irish History* (Oxford, 2014), pp. 113-4.
[100] *Nation*, 18 Aug. 1855.
[101] Alan O'Day, *Irish Home Rule, 1867-1921* (Manchester, 1998), p. 70.
[102] Duffy, *League of North and South*, p. 56.

concede that Lalor's resolutions at Holy Cross may also have helped to shape those principles, and in turn, influenced Gladstone's legislation.

Land reform, as defined by Crawford and Conner, involved adjustments to the existing structure of landlord/tenant relations, rather than a totally new system. Lalor favoured the latter because he believed that the existential questions raised by the Famine required radical, previously unthinkable, solutions. From January 1847 he engaged in an intensive campaign to win support from Irish Confederation leaders, but most were either lukewarm or hostile to his ideas. In his memoir of the period, Duffy recalled that Lalor's writings "made an intense impression" on three fellow Young Irelanders: Michael Doheny, Thomas Devin Reilly, and John Mitchel.[103] Doheny seems to have been the first member of the Confederation's council to meet Lalor and assisted him in organising the meeting at Holy Cross.[104] Reilly and Mitchel also became close associates of Lalor during 1847 and 1848. As Duffy implied, each in his own way was more open than most of the leadership to the radical course on which Lalor wished to take the Confederation.

Michael Doheny

Michael Doheny was co-organiser of the Holy Cross meeting held on 19 September 1847. As described in Chapter One, he vetoed Lalor's proposal for a rent-strike and used the event to restate the Confederation's support for the landowners and for the rights of private property. Such a stance seems oddly conservative for someone drawn to Lalor's bold ideas, but Doheny was more astute politically than the neophyte radical. His insistence that Lalor follow Irish Confederation policy was a tactical decision rather than a principled stand. He attempted to justify his stance in a letter to Lalor a few days after the Holy Cross event: "I think you will see now how valuable it was not to go the whole length on the first occasion."[105] Doheny was actually much closer to Lalor's thinking than his remarks at Holy Cross indicated. About a month after that event, *The Tipperary Vindicator* carried a report of an address made by Doheny and Lalor to worshippers outside a chapel near Templederry. According to the newspaper, the two men:

> commenced long and loud harangues on the rights of the tenant. The speeches were the same as those delivered at Holycross on the subject, but far more violent in their tone and tendency. Doheny told them "not to pay rent, nor taxes, but to keep their corn for their own use."[106]

---

[103] Duffy, *Four Years of Irish History*, p. 472.
[104] Ibid., p. 473.
[105] Doheny to JFL, 21 Sep. 1847, NLI, Ms. 340/26.
[106] *Tipperary Vindicator*, 20 Oct. 1847.

The account was provided by "a respectable correspondent in that locality" who went on to report that "the most respectable farmers turned away with disgust, and returned to their homes".[107] While some scepticism is warranted in evaluating what is clearly not an impartial source, it is quite feasible that Doheny would articulate such a radical message so soon after Holy Cross. At a meeting of the Irish Confederation held on 10 November, Doheny revealed to the assembly that, during the proceedings at Holy Cross, a letter arrived from John O'Connell. It contained O'Connell's admonition to the gathering not to withhold rent or rates. According to the press report of the Confederation meeting, Doheny then described what happened next:

> It was with feelings of the most intense gratification he (Mr. Doheny) witnessed a farmer tear the document from the wall on which it was posted and trample it under his feet with honest indignation (cheers).[108]

However, if Lalor was persuaded to tone down his rhetoric in order to win moderate support, he soon rebelled against what he regarded as the Confederation's continuing reluctance to follow his radical line and he cut off contact with Doheny.[109]

Despite the rift, Doheny's regard for Lalor and his teachings did not wane. Following the first of *The Irish Felon* articles[110], Doheny's response appeared in *The Irish Tribune*, the *Felon's* sister paper. In his letter, he described Lalor as "A man of rare capacity and wonderful power", and claimed that only slight differences separated the two men.[111] The tone of Doheny's letter is that of a somewhat reluctant acolyte, eager to demonstrate how closely his views align with those of his mentor, yet still keen to demonstrate his own intellectual autonomy. On the national question, Doheny set forth his position: "I regard a repeal of the union as a total abrogation, an utter and everlasting extinction of all English and imperial power in Ireland". His use of phrases such as "free republic" and "sovereign people" seemed to underline a commitment, shared with Lalor, "to the great end both of us have in view". On the other hand, Doheny could not easily set aside one important element of the union: the British monarch.

---

[107] Ibid.
[108] *Freeman's Journal*, 11 Nov. 1847.
[109] Ramón, *JFL*, pp. 27-8.
[110] *Irish Felon*, 24 Jun. 1848 (Ramón, *JFL*, pp. 96-108.)
[111] *Irish Tribune*, 1 July 1848.

I do not repudiate the queen, as Queen of Ireland, to administer Irish laws in the name, and behalf, and for the benefit of the Irish nation. No one questions her Majesty's claim to the crown of Ireland.

Aware that Lalor did not agree with the British crown having any role in an independent Ireland, Doheny qualified his stance by indicating his willingness to accept "a hereditary chief magistrate" as an alternative "guarant[or] of liberty". It could be argued that Doheny was trying here to give material expression to Lalor's "queen-metaphor". However, Lalor would place no earthly authority, whether monarch or magistrate, above the people. As he wrote in the article that prompted Doheny's letter, "the soil of Ireland for the people of Ireland, to have and to hold from God alone who gave it..."[112] It was to the soil that Doheny turned next in his response to Lalor's article.

Doheny agreed that "The property of Ireland is its soil; that soil belongs by divine right to all Irishmen..." He went further than this oft-stated principle by asserting that any land settlement should provide for the interest of "the majority of the people [who] occupy... no land". Moreover, Doheny echoed Lalor's uncompromising denunciation of landlords ("They or we must quit this island"), even though he had previously been more flexible on the subject. A few weeks earlier at a tenant right rally in County Down, Doheny declared that he "was not a leveller or an anarchist [who] sought... to take away his property from the landlord". On that occasion, he also upheld the landlord's right to his rent.[113] Now he proclaimed the necessity "that landlordism should be abolished whole and entire, name and nature, at once and for ever".[114] However, he stopped short of complete acceptance of Lalor's contention that the land belonged to "the nation at large, in full effective possession, to let to whom they will on whatever tenures, terms, rents, services, and conditions they will".[115] Instead, Doheny favoured a form of peasant proprietorship in which the state would act as an intermediary, collecting a tax from the new owners and paying it to their predecessors "for a certain number of years, until all claims of Irish owners would be satisfied".[116] Rather than the state becoming a permanent landlord, it would act as a temporary arbitrator between the new proprietors and the former landlords, ensuring that the latter received their compensation by instalments. In effect, Doheny anticipated the settlement made decades later by the Gladstone government and its successors.

---

[112] *Irish Felon*, 24 Jun. 1848 (Ramón, *JFL*, pp. 100-1.)
[113] *United Irishman*, 27 May 1848.
[114] *Irish Tribune*, 1 July 1848.
[115] *Irish Felon*, 24 Jun. 1848 (Ramón, *JFL*, p. 104.)
[116] *Irish Tribune*, 1 July 1848.

Whether, following the publication of Lalor's ideas on rent in "The Faith of a Felon", Doheny would have adjusted his thinking on these questions any further is impossible to judge. What is clear is that the "intense impression" described by Duffy did not last very long. Undoubtedly the dynamic pace of events during the following months played a significant part in this. A few weeks after publication of his letter, Doheny went on the run in the aftermath of the Ballingarry fracas and, by circuitous means, ended up in the United States where he spent the rest of his life.[117] Shortly after his arrival in America, he wrote and had published a book-length account of his involvement in the Irish nationalist movement between 1843 and 1848.[118] In it, he extolled the efforts made by one of his former associates to "compel the landlord class to some redeeming act of good sense and good will, which their own true interests required, as well as the agonies of the starving tenantry". Doheny went on to relate how the same colleague grew disenchanted with the landlords and came to regard "all further attempts to conciliate the upper classes... as foolish, feeble and cowardly", thus leading to his separation from the Confederation.[119] However Doheny was referring, not to James Fintan Lalor whose "vastly superior ability" he acknowledged in his *Tribune* letter a year earlier, but to the recently-transported John Mitchel. Doheny devoted almost an entire chapter of his book to Mitchel while barely mentioning Lalor.[120] Before exploring this seeming paradox any further, it is necessary to examine the relationship between Lalor and the second member of Duffy's triumvirate.

Thomas Devin Reilly

Although barely 23 years old when he first came to Lalor's attention, Thomas Devin Reilly (1824–54) was associated with the older man through both the *Nation* and *Irish Felon* periods.[121] Of all the members of the Confederation with whom he came into contact in 1847, Lalor regarded Reilly as one of his most ardent allies. In a letter to Mitchel, he singled out his correspondent as the only member of the Confederation on whom he could depend, "always excepting Devin Reilly". In the same letter Lalor referred to "two speeches [which Reilly had

---

[117] Desmond McCabe and James Quinn, "Doheny, Michael", *DIB* (Cambridge, 2009), (http://dib.cambridge.org/viewReadPage.do?articleId=a2655) 17 May 2018.
[118] Michael Doheny, *The Felon's Track* (New York, 1849).
[119] Ibid., pp. 74-5.
[120] Doheny's only reference was to Lalor's "daring principles and extraordinary ability", (*Felon's Track*, p. 87).
[121] James Quinn, "Reilly, Thomas Devin", *DIB* (Cambridge, 2009), (http://dib.cambridge.org/viewReadPage.do?articleId=a7626) 17 Jul. 2017.

made] at the Confederation". Clearly impressed by their content, Lalor wrote, "If the man be equal to the speeches—not always the case—he ought to be the foremost man of the Confederation".[122] An example of the rhetoric that provoked Lalor's praise was an address made by Reilly at a Confederation meeting on 22 April. His target was a government plan to induce 2,000,000 Irish people to move to Canada in order to alleviate the effects of the Famine.[123] Reilly urged those who might be relocated to "tell them [i.e. the landlords] that their place is not in the secret offices of the slaughtering alien, but on their own soil, at your head, consulting for your safety, and leading you to freedom".[124] Reilly's remarks echoed Lalor's own public entreaties to the landlords, while his harsher tone reflected the latter's private correspondence with the Confederation. As described in Chapter One, Reilly was one of the founders of both *The United Irishman* and *The Irish Felon*, and so continued to work closely with Lalor during 1848.[125] So aligned were the perspectives of the two men that an article now believed to have been written by Reilly for *The Irish Tribune* was attributed to Lalor in two of the early collections of the latter's writings.[126] In this piece, headlined "Rights of Labour", Reilly reiterated the principle of common property enunciated frequently by Lalor, "Every man is entitled to an equal share of the land, and all other things which are the free gift of nature".[127] However, he also approved of the rights of inheritance which "allows each individual to inherit the property of his father or other kinsman in lieu of the share to which he would be entitled of the general property".[128] Although he railed against "the landlord Thugs", Reilly did not follow Lalor in his call for a new society in which the land would be owned and administered by the people.[129]

Notwithstanding Lalor's admiration for his younger associate, Reilly—like Doheny—was much closer to John Mitchel. This is borne out by his emotional response to Mitchel's arrest and conviction for treason in May 1848. In an article in the first edition of *The Irish Felon*, he lambasted the viceroy, Lord

---

[122] JFL to Mitchel, 21 Jun. 1847, RIA 12.P.15/7.
[123] Peter Gray, *Famine, Land, and Politics: British Government and Irish Society, 1843-1850* (Dublin, 1999), pp. 300-1.
[124] *Nation*, 24 Apr. 1847.
[125] JFL to RL, 16 Jun. 1848 (est.), NLI, Ms. 8563/3. (Fogarty, *JFL*, pp. 116-7.)
[126] O'Donoghue, *JFL*, pp. 114-24. Marlowe, *JFL*, p. 105-13. In her 1918 collection, Fogarty questioned Lalor's authorship of the piece, citing P. S. O'Hegarty's analysis of the writing style, and concluding that it contained "few of the fine qualities of Lalor's prose" (p. 146). In his preface to the same collection, Griffith insisted that the piece was written by Reilly (p. xii).
[127] *Irish Tribune*, 1 July 1848.
[128] Ibid.
[129] Ibid.

Clarendon, for presiding over Mitchel's transportation, "I would wash the feet of that man before I would defile my hand with yours".[130] A month before that, in another heartfelt piece condemning Mitchel's arrest, this time in *The United Irishman*, Reilly attributed to his mentor some of the language and principles first conceived by Lalor:

> The soil of Ireland for the lives of the Irish people—the rule of Ireland by the will of the Irish people—the freedom of Ireland by the arms of the Irish people—these are his [i.e. Mitchel's] and theirs, one and indivisible.[131]

Like Doheny, Reilly fled to the United States in November 1848 following his participation in the failed Young Ireland rebellion earlier that year. During the remaining five years of his life, he made his living as a journalist on a number of Irish-American newspapers.[132] His journalistic interests centred on European and American politics, with no evidence of any lingering concern about the Irish land question.[133] However, in early-1850 he contributed an obituary to a New York newspaper following the news of Lalor's death.[134] In his tribute, Reilly did not mention either the private correspondence with the Irish Confederation to which he had been privy, or Lalor's contributions to *The Nation*. Instead, he implied that Lalor's brief career in journalism began, "upon the exile of Mr. Mitchel", with his contributions to *The Irish Felon*.[135]

As is clear from the foregoing analysis, Doheny and Reilly absorbed and accepted much of Lalor's thinking on the land question. Yet, even within Lalor's lifetime, both men publicly exalted John Mitchel as the source of those same policies and principles. To understand this anomaly, it is necessary to investigate the short but complex relationship that developed between Mitchel and Lalor during 1847 and 1848.

John Mitchel

There is no evidence that Lalor and John Mitchel ever met. Their association was founded on a correspondence that began on 9 March 1847 with Mitchel's

---

[130] *Irish Felon*, 24 Jun. 1848.
[131] *United Irishman*, 20 May 1848.
[132] Quinn, "Reilly, Thomas Devin".
[133] Sillard, *Life and Letters of John Martin*, pp. 88-104. John Mitchel, *Memoir of Thomas Devin Reilly: a lecture delivered by John Mitchel, in the Tabernacle, New-York, on Dec. 29th, 1856* (New York, 1857).
[134] *New York Tribune*, 1 Feb. 1850. (Byline: T.D.R.)
[135] Ibid.

first letter to Lalor.[136] These communications ended sometime in late-January or early-February of the following year.[137] In May 1848 Mitchel was arrested, convicted, and transported from Ireland.[138] The bulk of the correspondence that passed between them during those 10 or 11 months is lost. Two letters survive, one in its original manuscript form.[139] The other, a letter from Mitchel to Lalor dated 4 January 1848, was published in *The Irishman* several weeks after Lalor's death at the close of 1849.[140] Despite the paucity of first-hand sources, it is possible to reconstruct to some extent the relationship between Lalor and Mitchel through their other writings, as well as those left behind by mutual friends and associates.

When Lalor wrote his first letter to Duffy in January 1847, his concerns about the Young Irelanders' "imbecility" had not disappeared.[141] In fact, as Lalor wrote,

> …they have been terribly strengthened by the two last numbers of the "Nation"—I mean those of Dec 26 [1846] and January 2 [1847]; the last (Jan 9) I have not yet seen. It is not figure, but fact, that reading those two numbers made me ill.[142]

Duffy concluded in one of his memoirs that Lalor had been referring to two articles written by John Mitchel.[143] In the first of these, Mitchel tried to coax landlords into uniting against a new British government policy that would impose on them the financial burden of relieving the suffering caused by the Famine. Mitchel argued that self-interest should impel the landlords to make common cause with the people in "a national movement wherein the aristocracy of this land will hold its fit place".[144] In the second piece, Mitchel quoted from a letter published in several newspapers, including *The Nation*, from a landowner named Ralph Bernal Osborne.[145] In his letter, Osborne reiterated Mitchel's call for "a national movement" with the landlords at its head.[146] Mitchel believed that, in Osborne, he had found the man, "wise and

---

[136] JFL to Mitchel, 21 Jun. 1847, RIA 12.P.15/7.
[137] Ramón, *JFL*, p. 29.
[138] James Quinn, "Mitchel, John".
[139] JFL to Mitchel, 21 Jun. 1847, RIA 12.P.15/7.
[140] *Irishman*, 9 Feb. 1850. (also published in *Dundalk Democrat, Tuam Herald, Leinster Express,* and *Cork Examiner*, 13 Feb. 1850. See Fogarty, *JFL*, pp. 120-3.).
[141] Marnell to JFL, 6 Nov. 1846, NLI, Ms. 340/119.
[142] JFL to Duffy, 11 Jan. 1847, RIA 12.P.15/6.
[143] Duffy, *Four Years of Irish History*, p. 470, fn.
[144] *Nation*, 26 Dec. 1846.
[145] Ibid., 2 Jan. 1847.
[146] *Tipperary Vindicator*, 2 Jan. 1847.

bold and true... destined to lead his order", perhaps even towards the nationalist objective of repeal of the Act of Union.[147] In his letter to Duffy, Lalor did not elaborate on why Mitchel's articles had nauseated him, but it soon became clear to Duffy, Mitchel, and the other Young Irelanders that he did not share their faith in the landowners as potential allies in the cause of Irish independence. Nevertheless, as demonstrated in Chapter One, Lalor agreed to comply with the Confederation's policy as a temporary expedient.[148] Despite this, by his second *Nation* article he was excoriating the landlords for "their intention of serving notice to quit on the people of Ireland".[149] Moreover, far from viewing Osborne, as Mitchel did, as "an articulate voice to speak for those who can "give their thoughts no tongue'", Lalor rebuked the landowner by name as a proponent of the depopulation programme which he believed that he and his fellow landlords were engineering.[150]

Lalor's dissent from Mitchel's line is an early sign of the tension that persisted between the two men throughout their brief and turbulent relationship. Yet, in early 1847 at any rate, Mitchel was, in Duffy's recollection, "fascinated" by the arguments and ideas in Lalor's second letter, which Duffy circulated to his colleagues.[151] He alleged that Mitchel became so enraptured by Lalor's thinking, "that he adopted it in its entirety, as completely as a man adopts a new religion". Mitchel's reaction, Duffy maintained, represented "a deliberate reversal of all he had been preaching from his entry on public life down to the hour of its receipt".[152] Furthermore, according to Duffy, not only was Mitchel converted to Lalor's doctrines, he appropriated them as his own "without a single allusion to the author".[153] He cited Lalor's second letter, later published in *The Irish Felon*, as containing Mitchel's "political genesis".[154] A recent biographer has acknowledged that, while "Mitchel unquestionably appropriated some of Lalor's suppositions... Lalor [also] helped Mitchel clarify his own convictions".[155] Indeed, before he ever heard of Lalor, Mitchel was already articulating his dissatisfaction with the status quo.

---

[147] *Nation*, 2 Jan. 1847.
[148] *Irish Felon*, 1 Jul. 1848 (Ramón, *JFL*, p. 121.)
[149] *Nation*, 15 May 1847. (Ramón, *JFL*, p. 87.)
[150] Ibid.
[151] Duffy, *Four Years of Irish History*, p. 476.
[152] Ibid., p. 476.
[153] Duffy, *My Life in Two Hemispheres*, ii, p. 70.
[154] Ibid., ii, p. 80.
[155] Bryan P. McGovern, *John Mitchel: Irish Nationalist, Southern Secessionist* (Knoxville, 2009), p. 46.

One of Mitchel's first biographers has demonstrated through his analysis of *The Nation's* editorials that his subject was highly critical of the Irish land system from the moment he was appointed assistant editor in October 1845.[156] As the scale of the blight affecting the potato crop became clear that autumn, he warned "the land proprietors of this island" to acknowledge their tenants' diminished circumstances, otherwise "Irish landlordism has reached its latter days, and will shortly be with the feudal system and other effete institutions, in its grave".[157] Similarly, Mitchel was questioning landlord/tenant relations a year before Lalor's first article appeared in his newspaper. As famine spread Mitchel outlined a number of ways in which tenants could enjoy greater security in their holdings through some form of peasant proprietorship.[158] He concluded his editorial with a stark judgment that "the present system does not *work*", asking rhetorically if a better alternative could be found before society collapsed to "be born again out of the womb of chaos".[159] On the national question, Mitchel's position was often more extreme than that of his associates in the repeal movement. Even before he joined *The Nation*, Mitchel was contemplating physical force against Britain if repeal could not be won in any other way.[160] Later, as a main editorial writer for a national newspaper, his periodic calls for military action showed him to be much closer to the ideals of the United Irishmen, from whom Lalor later drew his inspiration, than to the non-violent agenda of the O'Connellites.[161]

As these examples illustrate, Mitchel's response to Lalor's ideas was not the "Damascene conversion" that Duffy depicted. It could be more accurately described as the recognition that passes between two individuals when they realise that they share, more or less, the same view of the world. If Mitchel was already harbouring an impulse to overturn the status quo, Lalor was offering him a plan and a set of principles to bring about a more equitable society. Yet, Mitchel seemed reluctant from the start to acknowledge publicly any debt he owed to Lalor for the insights which the latter brought to the Confederation.

When Lalor published his second letter to Duffy and his colleagues in *The Irish Felon* 18 months after he wrote it, he prefaced it with a short introduction. In it,

---

[156] William Dillon, *Life of John Mitchel* (2 vols, London, 1888), i, pp. 184-9.
[157] *Nation*, 25 Oct. 1845.
[158] *Nation*, 25 Apr. 1846.
[159] Ibid.
[160] "If Ireland be not ready to achieve the repeal with a strong hand, she ought to make herself ready without delay; and if she be worthy of the place she seeks among the nations, she will *do* that." (Mitchel to John Martin, Oct. 1843, quoted in Dillon, *John Mitchel*, i, p. 49.)
[161] *Nation*, 22 Nov. 1845.

he revealed that Mitchel had responded to the original stating that "he had fully adopted my views, and that he meant to act on them so soon as occasion should fit and serve".[162] Although Mitchel's letter is lost, it marked the beginning of the correspondence between the two men.[163] As Lalor's summary of the letter suggests, as of early-March 1847, Mitchel was not yet ready to put his newfound allegiance to Lalor's principles into practical effect. However, it did not prevent him from injecting a key plank of Lalor's hitherto privately-communicated strategy into one of his more militant contributions to *The Nation*. In May Mitchel threatened landlords with the prospect of either a bloody revolution or a mass rent-strike if they did not cooperate with the people.[164] At this point, Lalor was more concerned about mobilising the tenant farmers before the next harvest than of taking issue with Mitchel for revealing his rent-strike idea. So having chastised him for his reckless language, Lalor urged Mitchel to help him develop a planned campaign against the landlords, or else within "a few months... the star of Ireland has gone down for ever".[165] The ultimatum was necessary because, despite Mitchel's belligerent language, he continued to believe that the landlords could be "induced to do their duty by the people".[166] Lalor's entreaties worked. In August Lalor informed his brother that Mitchel had pledged his support for the Holy Cross event.[167] That support was not only moral or organisational. Luby later disclosed that, of the 12 pounds that Mitchel contributed to help defray the expenses of the meeting, 10 pounds came "out of his own pocket".[168]

Despite his verbal and financial support, Mitchel's backing for Lalor was not unqualified. In a letter to William Smith O'Brien, he expressed hope that the Holy Cross meeting would encourage the landlords to concede tenant right and thereby "take the people out of the hands of Lalor, and of all revolutionists".[169] By the following January, however, Mitchel admitted to Lalor that his faith in the landlords had been misplaced. This became clear two years later when Luby allowed a crucial letter from Mitchel to Lalor to be published; it formed part of the papers that Luby inherited on Lalor's death.[170] In the letter dated 4 January 1848, Mitchel expressed regret at not having done more to assist Lalor in the preparations for Holy Cross. He confessed "that on the only question we ever

---

[162] *Irish Felon*, 1 Jul. 1848. (Ramón, *JFL*, p. 113.)
[163] JFL to Mitchel, 21 Jun. 1847, RIA 12.P.15/7.
[164] *Nation*, 22 May 1847.
[165] JFL to Mitchel, 21 Jun. 1847, RIA 12.P.15/7.
[166] Dillon, *John Mitchel*, i, p. 169.
[167] JFL to RL, 21 Aug. 1847, NLI, Ms. 8563/2.
[168] *Irish Nation*, 17 Dec. 1881.
[169] Mitchel to O'Brien, 8 Sep. 1847, Fogarty, *JFL*, pp. 126-7.
[170] *Irishman*, 23 Feb. 1850.

differed about I was wholly wrong".[171] Mitchel was referring to the Confederation's failure to win landlord support for the modest reforms that he and his colleagues had proposed to them. In the same letter, Mitchel hinted that Lalor might join him and Devin Reilly in a new publishing venture. A more concrete offer followed shortly afterwards when Mitchel asked Lalor to contribute an article every two weeks to his soon-to-be-launched newspaper, *The United Irishman*, at a fee of 30 shillings per submission. According to Luby, Mitchel's offer sent Lalor into a "huff" and "the friendly relations between these two able Irishmen came to an end".[172]

As Mitchel's letter indicates, his disillusionment with the Confederation's policy of courting the landlords lagged Lalor's longstanding scepticism about their ever supporting repeal. In his letter to the Confederation of January 1847, Lalor referred to that policy as a temporary "experiment". As mentioned above, by his second article in *The Nation* a few months later, Lalor was declaring his "vote for resistance" to the landlords.[173] Even though he deferred to Doheny over the Holy Cross agenda, it is clear that by then Lalor's adhesion to the Confederation policy was purely cosmetic and against his better judgment. In February 1848 Mitchel delivered his last address at a Confederation meeting just before he resigned. In language redolent of Lalor's letter a year before, Mitchel told his colleagues that he had lost faith in the landlords:

> …it seems to have been always understood that our experiment upon the aristocracy was but an experiment, and must have an end some time or other.[174]

That Mitchel was now adopting Lalor's terminology may have been a face-saving exercise to justify his *volte face*. Nevertheless, it is ironic that, just when he and Lalor finally agreed on the principle that the landlords were to be opposed not nurtured, their relationship should end so abruptly. Fogarty was eloquent in her obituary for that relationship:

> They were, or could have been, completely complementary of each other. The one regret, the one disaster, the one germ of failure in them both, as in the movement for which they worked, sprang from the fact that they could not mingle forces in a common unity, for their common end.[175]

---

[171] Ibid., 9 Feb. 1850.
[172] *Irish Nation*, 17 Dec. 1881.
[173] *Nation*, 15 May 1847. (Ramón, *JFL*, p. 88.)
[174] Ibid., 5 Feb. 1848.
[175] Fogarty, *JFL*, pp. xxviii-xxix.

If Mitchel felt constrained in how he used Lalor's ideas before the final rift between them, he showed no such inhibitions afterwards. He had read Lalor's private letters to the Confederation leadership. Those additional letters addressed to him personally were, as Luby wrote in his memoirs, "mostly, I believe, on the land question".[176] As demonstrated in Chapter One, this private correspondence contained the fiery rhetoric which Lalor only made public more than a year later in the pages of *The Irish Felon*. In early 1848, however, if Irish nationalists knew anything about Lalor, it was that his contributions to *The Nation* and the newspaper accounts of the Holy Cross meeting revealed his position on repeal and the land question to be broadly in line with Irish Confederation policy. In fact, by the time Mitchel's new periodical began publication, it is likely that Lalor had been largely forgotten by most of its potential readers. If so they would have found nothing in *The United Irishman* to help them recall him or his writings. Throughout the little more than three months of that paper's history, nothing written by James Fintan Lalor appeared in its columns. Nor was his name even mentioned. However, in the tone, language, and content of Mitchel's leading articles, Lalor's inspiration and influence are evident, as several examples illustrate.

From his first contact with Duffy, Lalor made his disdain for the Confederation's repeal objective clear. This was a recurring theme of his private and public writings during 1847 and 1848. In his second letter of late-January 1847 (on which Duffy accused Mitchel of having based his new political philosophy), Lalor contended that "the small farmers and labourers [were] the only martial population that Ireland possesses". He then went on to explain why this army-in-waiting could not be counted on to fight for repeal.

> Their interest in it was never ardent; nor was it native or spontaneous, but forced and fictitious. Such as it was, it is now extinct, and can never be re-created.[177]

In his first letter to Duffy, Lalor used a colourful metaphor to make the same point:

> There is one [wolf-dog] at this moment in every cabin throughout the land, nearly fit already to be untied and he will be savager by-and-by. For Repeal, indeed he will never bite, but only bay…[178]

---

[176] *Irish Nation*, 17 Dec. 1881.
[177] *The Irish Felon*, 1 Jul. 1848 (Ramón, *JFL*, p. 117.)
[178] JFL to Duffy, 11 Jan. 1847, RIA 12.P.15/6.

That Mitchel had absorbed these points is clear from his second "Letter to the Protestant Farmers, Labourers, and Artizans, of the North of Ireland", published in *The United Irishman*.[179] Firstly, he paraphrased Lalor's argument that repeal did not inspire popular support:

> That [Grattan] Parliament is a very fine thing to talk or sing about; it has historic associations of a theatric sort; but no Irish peasant or working man will ever pull a trigger for the sake of restoring it.[180]

He then redefined repeal in the primal language perfected by Lalor:

> [Irish repealers] want a home, and a foot-hold on the soil, that they may not be naked and famishing beggars in their own land. In one word, they demand Ireland *for the Irish*—not for the Irish gentry alone.[181]

In a sequel to this published letter, written shortly before his arrest, Mitchel demonstrated his total acceptance of Lalor's concept of popular and national autonomy:

> My friends, the People's Sovereignty: the land, and sea, and air of Ireland, for the People of Ireland: this is the gospel that the Heavens and the earth are preaching, and that all hearts are secretly burning to embrace. Give up for ever that old interpretation you put upon the word "Repeal". Repeal is... not a local legislature,—not a return to "our ancient Constitution,"—not a golden link, or patchwork Parliament, or a College-green chapel-of-ease to Saint Stephens's—but an Irish Republic, one and indivisible.[182]

Mitchel even articulated Lalor's principle of a common stake in the land shared by rural and urban dwellers alike:

> the working men—the tillers of the field and the artificers of the workshop—own all the wealth of the state; and that no one else owns anything, as no one else creates anything. That they are owners of the state—its sovereigns and masters.[183]

If Lalor's deployment of his queen-metaphor failed to move most of his Young Ireland associates, Mitchel embraced it. Shortly before his arrest for sedition, he publicly rejected any form of Irish self-government that involved "loyalty to

---

[179] *United Irishman*, 29 Apr. 1848.
[180] Ibid.
[181] Ibid.
[182] Ibid., 13 May 1848.
[183] Ibid., 15 Apr. 1848.

Queen Victoria".[184] A few weeks later, he was on his way to exile on board the *Shearwater*. He recorded in his *Jail Journal* that, as he gazed on the receding shoreline of his native land, he mourned his separation from Ireland, "my mother and queen!'[185]

During the last half-century of his long life, Charles Gavan Duffy seldom let an opportunity slip of reminding his readers that John Mitchel had "masquerade[ed] in the stolen garments of Fintan Lalor".[186] The allegation appeared first in a supplement to *The Nation* of 15 April 1854, later published separately as a pamphlet.[187] The supplement took the form of an open letter in which Duffy responded to charges laid against him by Mitchel in his recently-published *Jail Journal*.[188] Despite being arrested in 1848, Duffy was not convicted of sedition and became the only leading Young Irelander to avoid prison or exile.[189] Mitchel followed events in Ireland from his confinement abroad and was irate at the inconclusive outcome of Duffy's two trials, a result he attributed to the accused's "miserable grovelling".[190] During his captivity, Mitchel's attitude to Duffy grew increasingly hostile and he poured his feelings into his journal, going so far as to apply the insulting soubriquet, "Mr Give-in Duffy", to his former employer.[191] Following the publication of Mitchel's remarks, Lalor became a weapon in the ill-tempered exchanges between the two newspapermen.[192] Not only did Duffy accuse Mitchel of plagiarising the ideas of their now-deceased colleague, he claimed that Lalor himself had confided his "indignation" at this when the two men were imprisoned together in 1848.[193] In his serialised memoir of those febrile times, Luby corroborated Duffy's recollection, writing that Lalor "felt more or less embittered against John Mitchel… accus[ing] him of appropriating his ideas".[194] Mitchel himself was unrepentant, however. Following Duffy's charge of plagiarism, Mitchel made a forthright admission in the pages of *The Citizen*: "Yes: I adopted

---

[184] Ibid., 13 May 1848.
[185] John Mitchel, *Jail Journal, or, Five years in British prisons* (New York, 1854), p. 24.
[186] Duffy, *My Life in Two Hemispheres*, ii, p. 70.
[187] Charles Gavan Duffy, *Letter to John Mitchel* (Dublin, 1854).
[188] Mitchel absconded from his Tasmanian exile in November 1853 and moved to New York where, in the following January, he set up a new weekly newspaper, *The Citizen*. Extracts from his *Jail Journal* were published in *The Citizen* before it appeared in book form.
[189] Steven R. Knowlton, "The quarrel between Gavan Duffy and John Mitchel: implications for Ireland", *Albion: A Quarterly Journal Concerned with British Studies*, 21/4 (1989), p. 581.
[190] Mitchel, *Jail Journal*, p. 162.
[191] Ibid., p. 306.
[192] Knowlton, "Quarrel between Gavan Duffy and John Mitchel", pp. 589-90.
[193] *Nation*, 27 May 1854.
[194] *Irish Nation*, 17 Dec. 1881.

Lalor's opinions: I called them my own: I preached and acted upon them..." However, he would not accept that Lalor "grudged me the ideas I took from him".[195]

Although Mitchel drew freely upon Lalor's doctrines and principles, he demurred when it came to the final settlement of the land question. While the two men differed for a time in their respective approaches to handling the landowning class, on the question of land tenure their disagreement was more fundamental. Yet for reasons that are unclear, both men chose to understate this. In his introduction to the published version of his second letter to Duffy, Lalor wrote only that "between [Mitchel] and myself there was from the first an *almost* perfect agreement".[196] Writing to O'Brien in August 1847, Mitchel disclosed that regarding "the ultimate settlement of the tenure question... my doctrine is *nearly* identical with Lalor's".[197] In another letter to O'Brien sent shortly before the meeting at Holy Cross, Mitchel informed the Confederation leader that, in his planning for the setting up of a tenant league in Tipperary, Lalor "does not now go for the whole of his system".[198] The allusion to "the whole of his system" indicates that, through their correspondence, Mitchel had gained some understanding of Lalor's radical proposals to resolve the land question. His rejection of those proposals may explain the use of the qualifying adverbs, "almost" and "nearly", in the correspondence cited above.

As his own writings on the subject demonstrate, Mitchel upheld the principle of private property in land and never accepted Lalor's proposal to make land a common resource vested in the people at large. Nonetheless, traces of Lalor's influence can be detected in Mitchel's first significant attempt to delve more deeply into the issue of land tenure. Sometime in 1847, Mitchel undertook desk research into the landholding systems operating in various European countries. He presented his findings to his colleagues in October and his lectures were published in pamphlet form in the following year.[199] Like Lalor, Mitchel emphasised the role of tenant farmers in the national struggle for independence, "Whether Ireland is to become a free nation or no, depends upon the way in which our garrison of farmers acquit themselves, and stand upon the rights of property".[200] On the other hand, while he deplored the attitude of "absolute" ownership which some Irish landlords displayed, he did not share Lalor's interest in "abstract questions on the 'rights of property,' or the origin or nature of

---

[195] *Citizen*, 6 May 1854.
[196] *Irish Felon*, 1 Jul. 1848 (Ramón, *JFL*, p. 114.) Emphasis in original.
[197] Mitchel to O'Brien, 8 Aug. 1847, Fogarty, *JFL*, pp. 125-6. Emphasis added.
[198] Mitchel to O'Brien, 8 Sep. 1847, Fogarty, *JFL*, pp. 126-7.
[199] John Mitchel, *Lectures on the Land Tenures of Europe* (Dublin, 1848)
[200] Ibid., p. 4.

ownership in the soil".²⁰¹ Mitchel's European survey uncovered little approximating to Lalor's ideal of popular sovereignty over the land, with every farmer a tenant of the people.²⁰² Instead, "you find everywhere that the peasants are either owners of the land they till, or are somehow or other secured a permanency of tenure…"²⁰³ Although Mitchel's research stretched across the continent, from France to Russia, he devoted most of his attention to Prussia.

In the wake of its defeat by Napoleon at Jena in 1806, Prussia under its monarch, Frederick William III, undertook a series of wide-ranging political, economic and social reforms. These were driven by two successive chancellors of the king, Karl Freiherr von Stein, and August Prince von Hardenberg. The effect of their reform of the land laws was to make it possible for tenants to buy their farms and thus become peasant proprietors.²⁰⁴ In the period leading up to the Great Famine, Prussian land reforms became a touchstone for critics of Ireland's land system.²⁰⁵ An early editorial in *The Nation*, probably by Davis, also invoked Stein and Hardenberg's land reforms, against which "no one but the Prussian nobles murmured". This was, the writer asserted, an example of how to "revolutionise by law" in order to benefit the peasant.²⁰⁶ In his survey of European land tenures, Mitchel continued in this vein, declaring "that far the greater part of Prussia is now in the hands of peasant proprietors".²⁰⁷ If the Battle of Jena had been the spur to the reform programme initiated by Prussia's rulers, Mitchel argued that Ireland's Jena, i.e. the Famine, would not provoke the same result, "unless the survivors of the people take the affair into their own hands".²⁰⁸ So while Mitchel was clearly influenced by Lalor's three-way association of the peasantry, repeal, and the Famine, he rejected his erstwhile

---

²⁰¹ Ibid., pp. 30-1.
²⁰² Mitchel briefly alluded to Turkey where "the peasants are proprietors of the land they till, and pay only a tax to the state" (p. 17). Although agricultural land in Turkey was theoretically vested in the state, in practice a landlord/tenant system operated at the time of Mitchel's research leading to "exploitation of the peasants and the lands". (Fatma Gül Ünal, *Land Ownership Inequality and Rural Factor Markets in Turkey: a Study for Critically Evaluating Market Friendly Reforms* (New York, 2012), p. 21).
²⁰³ Mitchel, *Land Tenures of Europe*, p. 18.
²⁰⁴ Jonathan Sperber, "The Atlantic revolutions in the German lands, 1776–1849", in Helmut Walser Smith (ed.), *The Oxford Handbook of Modern German history* (Oxford, 2011), pp. 155-6.
²⁰⁵ R. D. Collison Black, *Economic Thought and the Irish Question, 1817-1870* (Cambridge, 1960), p. 57. (See also Raumer, *England in 1835*, iii, p. 200-1.)
²⁰⁶ *Nation*, 23 Dec. 1843.
²⁰⁷ Mitchel, *Land Tenures of Europe*, p. 28.
²⁰⁸ Ibid., p. 34.

associate's untested concept of communal land ownership in favour of the individual proprietorship to be found in continental Europe.

During the first half of 1848, Mitchel repeatedly expounded his views on the Irish land question through his new periodical, *The United Irishman*. His articles on the subject demonstrate that Mitchel continued to favour individual property rights. He promoted a settlement that would give tenant farmers a more secure stake in their holdings, what he called "a joint proprietorship in the fee-simple of the land".[209] Once again citing Prussia as a model, he claimed that Ireland could unlock its agricultural potential through the creation of "innumerable small capitalists, eager to invest their money in the land".[210] Despite everything, he held out hope of a peaceful resolution, "with *compensation* for vested interests!" If the landlords resisted, however, they would be "scourged...from the face of the land for ever'.[211] By early May 1848, Mitchel was leaning towards the latter option. "I have advised that the people... should take the law into their own hands", he proclaimed, "and defend their lives and properties by combining together for active and passive resistance". On the tenure question, it seemed to make little difference to him whether success in that struggle led to its participants holding their land as tenants who enjoyed security and fair rent, or as proprietors who paid no rent at all.[212]

Even as he languished in his tropical prison in the autumn of 1848, Mitchel remained under Lalor's spell. In an entry to his *Jail Journal*, he expressed ideas and concepts that were central to Lalor's thinking, employing language that owed much to their source:

> Property is an institution of Society not a Divine endowment, whose title-deed is in heaven... but when matters come to that utterly intolerable condition in which they have long been in Ireland, Society itself stands dissolved—a fortiori—property is forfeited... There has come, for that nation, an absolute need to re-construct Society, to re-organise Order and Law, to put property into a course whereby it will re-distribute itself...[213]

Yet, although he continued to receive news and newspapers from Ireland, Mitchel never mentioned or referred to Lalor in his journal. Indeed, apart from the references in *The Citizen* prompted by Duffy's criticisms, Lalor's name rarely

---

[209] *United Irishman*, 26 Feb. 1848.
[210] Ibid.
[211] Ibid., 1 Apr. 1848.
[212] Ibid., 6 May 1848.
[213] Mitchel, *Jail Journal*, p. 79.

appeared in Mitchel's subsequent published writings.[214] Unlike Duffy and John O'Leary for example, he did nothing to preserve and pass on Lalor's teachings on the land question to future generations of nationalists. For Mitchel, it seems that Lalor's doctrines and principles were a free resource to be appropriated and adapted as prevailing circumstances demanded, without any reference to the memory or reputation of their progenitor.[215] Mitchel was, as one modern scholar has described him, "most effective as a synthesiser and populariser of the ideas of others, rather than as an original thinker in his own right".[216] Unlike Lalor, who became a progressive-minded theorist when circumstances forced him to confront his conservative values, Mitchel was essentially a reactionary figure. Militant nationalist though he was, before and after his acquaintanceship with Lalor, Mitchel remained, as Dillon put it, "much more conservative than radical [and] averse to change…"[217]

Despite, or because of, these characteristics, Mitchel's impact on the more radical of his Young Ireland associates was stronger and more long-lasting than Lalor's. Following Duffy's public attack on Mitchel, one of those who came to his defence was Doheny. Perhaps tellingly, in his letter of support for Mitchel, Doheny did not refer at all to Lalor or to the charge of plagiarism. Instead, he focused his indignation and ire on "Mr. Duffy's miserable libel", contrasting it with Mitchel's "proud defiance" in the dock.[218] But for the fact that he had died barely two months earlier in Washington DC, it is quite probable that Devin Reilly would have added to the encomiums in support of Mitchel published in *The Citizen*, while simultaneously ignoring Lalor. Doheny and Reilly's support for Mitchel's unashamed usurpation of Lalor's ideas reflects the changing dynamics in Irish nationalism that followed the events of 1848. From the time he was arrested in May, Mitchel's case attracted the sympathy of even the most moderate of nationalists, such as John O'Connell.[219] The editorial writer of *The*

---

[214] A single reference can be found in *The Last Conquest of Ireland (perhaps)* (1860), p.195, to "James Fintan Lalor of Kildare county (sic)… [who] was the most powerful political writer that our cause had yet called forth, if I except Davis only".

[215] Despite Mitchel's admission in the pages of *The Citizen* (see above), Dillon rejected the charge of "any unfair or dishonourable appropriation by Mitchel of Lalor's ideas". (see Dillon, *John Mitchel*, i, p. 152)

[216] Andrew Shields, "From repeal to revolution: the evolution of John Mitchel's political thought 1843–48", in Anders Ahlqvist and Pamela O'Neill (eds.), *Language and Power in the Celtic World: papers from the seventh Australian Conference of Celtic Studies, University of Sydney, September 2010* (Sydney, 2010), p. 422.

[217] Dillon, *John Mitchel*, i, p. xv.

[218] *Citizen*, 6 May 1854.

[219] *United Irishman*, 27 May 1848.

Freeman's Journal was fulsome in his praise of Mitchel's bearing in the courtroom, "Bold without bluster, he met his fate in a manner worthy [of] his chivalrous character".[220] As a recent biographer noted, "After his conviction, Mitchel would begin to assume the figure of martyr".[221] For Lalor, however, there was no heroic moment, either in the dock or on the battlefield, which might have won the fealty of Young Irelanders such as Doheny and Reilly. Lalor did not, or could not, attract the kind of personal devotion that such men felt for Mitchel.[222] Lenihan described his old schoolmate as "sickly, restless, and irritable", not characteristics designed to inspire popular support as, for instance, the outcome at Holy Cross demonstrates.[223]

Crucially, Mitchel's recycling of Lalor's ideas on repeal and the land question appeared in the public domain before Lalor himself outlined the full extent of his thinking in *The Irish Felon*. Thus it must have seemed that Lalor was merely reiterating Mitchel's position rather than articulating his own carefully-worked out philosophy. As the writings of Doheny and Reilly cited above illustrate, this was an impression that associates and admirers of Mitchel seemed willing to foster. Other examples confirm this. An editorial in *The Irishman* eulogised Mitchel as "the first truth-teller for a long time", and asserted that "his pen made [the] importance [of the land question] understood".[224] In his 1856 history of recent Irish uprisings, John Savage claimed that Lalor "did not publicly enter political life until after Mitchel's banishment".[225] Even the young Luby was caught up in the outpouring of pro-Mitchel fervour that followed his trial and transportation. In an article published after he released some of the correspondence between Mitchel and Lalor, Luby referred to the latter as "the chief writer of the *Felon*, the principles of which were an echo of those of the *United Irishman*".[226] Dying in obscurity as he did at the tail end of 1849, Lalor's part in shaping Young Ireland's role at the forefront of Irish nationalism seemed destined to be relegated to that of a supporting player to John Mitchel's main performance. Although this interpretation has persisted in the historiography, as outlined in Chapter One, it was to some extent rectified when Lalor's writings were republished later in the century.

---

[220] *Freeman's Journal*, 29 May 1848.
[221] McGovern, *John Mitchel*, p. 85.
[222] In a letter to Mitchel received in January 1853, Devin Reilly revealed that he had named his recently-deceased son after his friend. (Mitchel, *Jail Journal*, p. 301.)
[223] *Tipperary Vindicator*, 26 Apr. 1867.
[224] *Irishman*, 8 Sep. 1849.
[225] Savage, *'98 and '48*, p. 343-4.
[226] *Irishman*, 23 Feb. 1850.

Readers of *The Nation* and *The Irish Felon*

Very few records have survived of the impact that Lalor's articles in *The Nation* and *The Irish Felon* made on the many readers they attracted. A year after its launch, Duffy's newspaper was outselling its main Dublin rivals, whether they were published daily, weekly, or less often. In 1844 sales of *The Nation* exceeded 8,600.[227] The newspaper was circulated in virtually every town and village throughout the country, and Duffy estimated that the actual readership may have reached a quarter-of-a-million.[228] By 1847, when Lalor's contributions began to appear, sales had fallen to a little over 5,000, but they still managed to outstrip those of its nearest rival, *The Weekly Freeman*.[229] During its short run, *The Irish Felon* was also a success, with official sales figures calculated at over 9,000, comfortably ahead of the other Dublin weeklies, including the *Freeman*.[230] However, because of official harassment of the radical press during 1848, circulation outside Dublin was erratic.[231] Nevertheless Lalor's articles in both papers—each piece bearing his full name as the by-line—reached numerous Irish readers with nationalist sympathies. Unfortunately, however, the letters and diaries that might have yielded insight into how those articles were received at the time are unavailable or lost, leaving scholars to make do with mostly scraps of circumstantial and anecdotal evidence. Insofar as that evidence reveals anything, it is that Lalor's writings generated a largely positive response from the nationalist-leaning public, as the following examples illustrate.

According to O'Neill, many of Lalor's fellow prisoners during his imprisonment in Newgate "had a high regard for his opinions" as displayed in his writings.[232] In one of his newspaper memoirs Luby recalled that, while staying at a Limerick hotel during the summer of 1849, he overheard "a tall, clever-looking lady... fast verging on middle age", quoting to her friends from one of Lalor's *Irish Felon* pieces, "the land from the sky to the centre".[233] To these brief anecdotes can be added the press accounts of Lalor's funeral. The details, e.g. a line of mourners "four deep... [that] extended the whole length of Sackville Street", and the coffin being carried "on the shoulders of the citizens" from the city centre to Glasnevin cemetery, suggest a high level of popular support for Lalor, in Dublin at least.[234]

---

[227] Andrews, *Newspapers and Newsmakers*, p. 27.
[228] Ibid., p. 23.
[229] Ibid., p. 27.
[230] Tally, "Dublin weekly press", p. 160.
[231] Ibid., p. 188.
[232] O'Neill, *JFL*, p. 93.
[233] *Irish Nation*, 14 Apr. 1883.
[234] *Freeman's Journal*, 31 Dec. 1849, 1 Jan. 1850.

Although it cannot be determined if this support was founded on what *The Freeman's Journal* referred to as "his peculiarly able articles on the land question", it is perhaps significant that he was honoured in death by urban-dwellers who would have benefited from the rent proposal he set out in "The Faith of a Felon".[235]

Yet, if Lalor's doctrine of communal control over the land stirred much interest in his readers, there is virtually no evidence to confirm it. Of the 16 extant letters sent by readers to *The Irish Felon* office following his first three articles in that periodical, only one correspondent, Michael Segrave an Irish-born Chartist who lived in Barnsley, Yorkshire, alluded to his comments on the land question.[236] In his letter, Segrave declared both his desire to "repeal the Conquest", and his support for radical land reform. He outlined his belief "that rights of property in land ought to be entirely abolished... [and that] no class of men ought to be allowed to claim as their own what was not produced by the hands of man..." Segrave wrote in a tone indicative of one who had found a kindred spirit with similar views to his own. Almost two years later in an open letter to the Chartist leader, Feargus O'Connor, published in *The Irishman*, Segrave echoed Lalor's essential argument against exclusive, individual ownership of property in land:

> God created the land, and gave it to the whole people as their inheritance; and those who have taken it by force are robbers of one of God's choicest gifts; and those who purchase it from those same robbers are, at best, nothing better than receivers of stolen goods.[237]

Although in the same letter Segrave revealed that he had once supported O'Connor, his own thinking on land tenure was closer to that of Bronterre O'Brien.[238] Segrave's response to *The Irish Felon* articles is therefore a reminder of how closely aligned were the positions of Lalor and O'Brien on this question. However, as demonstrated in Chapter Two, circumstances were never propitious for any association between these two land reformers.

***

When Lalor began his association with the Young Irelanders, his goal was not to bring fame and glory on his own head as a nationalist hero. He sought to influence those already in the vanguard of the struggle against British rule, and who had the means to reach the wider nationalist population. When he had gained their attention, Lalor urged Young Ireland to develop its own distinctive

---

[235] Ibid., 29 Dec. 1849.
[236] NLI, Ms. 340/152.
[237] *Irishman*, 27 Apr. 1850.
[238] Ibid.

platform by channelling the widespread disaffection among tenant farmers into a mass movement that could fulfil the aims of the United Irishmen. Lalor's message was unsettling for the moderates within Young Ireland, but it helped to radicalise Mitchel and his circle. However, in the frenzied atmosphere that overtook nationalist Ireland during 1848, Lalor himself was largely overlooked, even by those on whom his writings had the greatest impact. One of the very few who appreciated Lalor's true contribution was his *Irish Felon* colleague, Joseph Brenan. In a generous tribute published in the United States and Ireland following Lalor's death, Brenan made it known that Lalor had not simply sprung from Mitchel's shadow in the summer of 1848.[239] Although he concurred with his fellow nationalists that Lalor "was not prominent in Irish politics until John Mitchel had struggled and fell", Brenan described how his late colleague had been "working under-ground" before this.

> He corresponded with all the men who *were* prominent; gave them advice and supplied them with ideas. He was a revolutionist even in the 'peaceful, legal, and constitutional' day, and only wanted position and power to rebuild Ireland from her ruins.[240]

Despite the evidence that Mitchel's failure to acknowledge his influence upset him, Lalor was much more concerned to see his country freed from foreign domination. That became his primary goal during the last 18 months or so of his life. As demonstrated in Chapter Two, while Lalor's theory of land as the "common property of all mankind" was not new, his application of it to Ireland as he saw it in the late-1840s was unique and radical. Having said that, he could not have fashioned his doctrines without the lessons he learnt from two key figures in his early life. The first was his father, Patt Lalor, who demonstrated how one man could alter the status quo through pursuing a well-thought-out plan that attracted widespread popular support. The other was William Conner, Lalor's mentor during his initial engagement with the land question. From Conner, he undoubtedly gained a wider experience of the deficiencies of Irish land tenure than he could ever have gleaned at Tinakill. As detailed above Lalor failed to persuade either of his early teachers that his ideas deserved careful consideration as an improvement on their own proposals. In truth, however, even the most progressive of nationalist leaders were not ready for the revolutionary leap in landholding that Lalor advocated. Nevertheless, his insights into the defects of the contemporary land system did leave their mark on the subsequent thinking of both moderate and extremist wings of Young Ireland. Perhaps surprisingly it was the conservative Duffy who tried to

---

[239] Ibid., 16 Mar. 1850.
[240] Ibid.

implement Lalor's land strategy, albeit the Holy Cross version, after its author's death. Although the more radical Mitchel, Doheny, and Reilly went some way towards acceptance of Lalor's unadulterated theories of land tenure, even they baulked at any provision that might undermine the rights of private property. Mostly, however, Lalor's concepts were either ignored or rejected by his contemporaries, whether they were family, friends or fellow-activists in the cause of land reform.

Epilogue

In the decades that followed Lalor's death, his dream of a free republic, in which the nation's land would be at the disposal of the people, was largely forgotten. His memory was revived with the formation of the National Land League of Mayo on 16 August 1879, a precursor to the Irish National Land League founded two months later.[1] In his address at the inaugural meeting of the Mayo body, co-founder Michael Davitt paraphrased Lalor when he outlined its main principle:

> The land of Ireland belongs to the people of Ireland, to be held and cultivated for the sustenance of those whom God decreed to be the inhabitants thereof.[2]

As described in the preceding chapters, this precept was subject to differing interpretations by land reformers and others. For Lalor, however, the meaning was clear and having previously equivocated over his true position, he gave it its fullest expression in "The Faith of a Felon". Davitt, described as "the spiritual heir of James Fintan Lalor", not only accepted Lalor's perspective, he openly promulgated land nationalisation just as the move towards peasant proprietorship was gathering momentum.[3] In 1904, when Davitt came to recount the achievements of the Land League, he expressed his regret that Lalor had not launched his "revolutionary nationalist uprising" in 1847. From the vantage point of more than half-a-century later, Davitt pondered how Ireland's history might have been altered as a result.

> ...there would have been less loss of life, less national shame to lament over in after years, while there would have been a far speedier settlement of the land and national questions.[4]

That neither question had been settled to Davitt's satisfaction was obvious[5] Instead of the nationalisation of Ireland's land, ownership of many thousands

---

[1] Foster, *Modern Ireland*, p. 404.
[2] *Freeman's Journal*, 18 Aug. 1879.
[3] John E. Pomfret, *The Struggle for Land in Ireland, 1800-1923* (Princeton, 1930), p. 108. R.V. Comerford, "The Land War and the politics of distress, 1877–82", in W.E. Vaughan (ed.), *A New History of Ireland, Volume VI: Ireland Under the Union, II: 1870-1921* (Oxford, 2010), pp. 21-2.
[4] Michael Davitt, *The Fall of Feudalism in Ireland or the Story of the Land League Revolution* (London, 1904), p. 58.
[5] Paul Bew, "The Land League ideal: achievements and contradictions", in P. J. Drudy (ed.), *Ireland: Land, Politics and People* (Cambridge, 1982), p. 84. Comerford, "Land war and the politics of distress", pp. 21-2.

of farms was transferred from a small number of landlords to a new class of peasant proprietors.[6] Moreover, this "social revolution", as Philip Bull dubbed it, was effected, not by an independent Irish government, but through legislation enacted in the British parliament.[7] Bull described the outcome:

> Ireland was now dominated by small capitalist peasant proprietors, their interests distinctly different from when they had been tenants...[8]

Davitt realised that the prospect of a rebellion of the landless—Lalor's "prepared, organised, and resistless revolution"—was now a dead letter. As O'Neill put it, "It is unusual for property owners to riot".[9] The land question may have been settled but in a way that left the national question unresolved. In June 1848 Lalor expressed his "wish... to combine and cement the two [questions] into one; and so, perfect, and reinforce, and carry both".[10] That connection, which he forged with his "railway carriage" analogy, offered a radical solution to Ireland's ills. The severing of that link began in the early 1850s with the advent of Charles Gavan Duffy's Tenant League. The land bills enacted later by successive British governments sundered it forever.

---

[6] Paul Bew, *Conflict and Conciliation in Ireland, 1890-1910: Parnellites and Radical Agrarians* (Oxford, 1987), p. 136.
[7] Philip Bull, *Land, Politics and Nationalism: a Study of the Irish Land Question* (Dublin, 1996), p. 24.
[8] Ibid., p. 173.
[9] O'Neill, *JFL*, p. 120. For a different perspective see Timothy McMahon, "'The land for the people': the Irish Revolution as a revolution of rising expectations" in Michael De Nie and Sean Farrell (eds.), *Power and Popular Culture in Modern Ireland: Essays in Honour of James S. Donnelly, Jr.* (Dublin, 2010), pp. 172-92.
[10] *Irish Felon*, 24 Jun. 1848. (Ramón, *JFL*, p. 103.)

Conclusion

The fact that the substance of Lalor's thinking has never been put into practice should not detract from the potency of his writings. Part of the reason why they have been reprinted and republished almost continuously during the last century and more lies in Lalor's mastery of the written word. He understood that his abilities were not those of a charismatic leader, like Daniel O'Connell, whose oratory could sway the crowd. Joseph Brenan recalled an observation made by Lalor about himself: "'Here in a public meeting", I once heard him say, "I am a unit, but pen in hand I am a unit with two noughts after it'".[1] His old school friend Maurice Lenihan noted, "…as a public writer, [he] was beyond all question, one of the ablest, most trenchant, and accomplished, of his time".[2] In the last of his four reflections on Irish nationalism, Patrick Pearse made the same point more pithily: "No one who wrote as little as Lalor has ever written so well".[3] However, Lalor's writings could not have endured purely on the basis of their literary qualities.

Pearse understood Lalor's philosophy better than most of his contemporary or later admirers.[4] This extract from Pearse's final essay, written only weeks before the Easter Rising, illustrates how keenly he grasped Lalor's concept of the bond between the land and the people.

> The essence of Lalor's teaching is that the right to the material ownership of a nation's soil co-exists with the right to make laws for the nation and that both are inherent in the same authority, the Sovereign People. He held in substance that Separation from England would be valueless unless it put the people—the actual people and not merely certain rich men—of Ireland in effectual ownership and possession of the soil of Ireland…[5]

Lalor was convinced that, if this teaching were to be realised, Ireland would become an exemplar for other oppressed nations. He did not consider his proposed rent strike solely as a short-term weapon to help end British hegemony. It would be the basis of an "earthquake" that could spread from Ireland throughout Europe, just as the French Revolution had done. Turning a local rent strike into an international revolutionary act indicates the breadth and boldness of Lalor's

---

[1] *Irishman*, 16 Mar. 1850.
[2] *Tipperary Vindicator*, 26 Apr. 1867.
[3] Padraic Pearse, "The Sovereign People" in *Collected Works of Padraic H. Pearse: Political Writings and Speeches* (Dublin, 1922), p. 346.
[4] R. Uí Chollatáin, "P. H. Pearse deeply influenced by writings of James Fintan Lalor", *Laois Heritage Society Journal*, 3/ (2006), pp. 24-35.
[5] Pearse, *Collected Works*, p. 350.

vision, especially at a time when Davis and Mitchel were content merely to promote systems of land tenure operating elsewhere.

There are several reasons why Lalor did not develop his principles of landholding and national self-determination into a detailed blueprint. The main obstacle was the increasingly chaotic state of the country as it was overwhelmed by the Famine and the revolutionary tide that swept across Europe. The rapidly-changing conditions took Lalor away from the rural isolation where he had conceived his ideas into the fractious world of nationalist politics and insurrection. Of course, Lalor's death at only 42, before the Famine had run its course, ended any prospect of him resuming his career as a radical thinker and polemicist. So we do not know how he would have turned his theories into a practical plan of action. Nevertheless, as I have argued in this study, Lalor's surviving writings contain several important elements that fit together into a coherent and farsighted philosophy. Those elements are: 1) national independence to encompass not only political autonomy but also control over the land, vesting ultimate ownership in the entire people as "lords paramount", 2) all citizens, urban and rural dwellers alike, to benefit economically from the produce of the land, 3) a relationship of equals to be negotiated between a sovereign Irish republic and Great Britain, 4) Ireland to join France as international models of a new popular spirit spawned by the 1789 revolution.

By combining "the national sentiment with the agrarian interest" James Fintan Lalor represented, in Michael Davitt's mind, Ireland's best hope of national salvation during the depths of the Famine.[6] However, Lalor's legacy should not be judged on his failed attempt to instigate a rebellion in support of independence and control of the land. Given the scale of opposition to his plans by both mainstream Irish nationalism and the British establishment, and the sheer carnage being wrought by the Famine, a mass uprising of the kind Lalor envisaged was most unlikely. Lalor's true legacy lies in his ideas about Ireland, its land, and its people. Despite the specific circumstances in which they first appeared in print, those ideas have lost none of their "freshness and force" for successive generations of Irish people.

Bronterre O'Brien and others may have arrived at conclusions on landholding similar to Lalor's, but their rationale had nothing to do with a radical reinterpretation of feudal law, nor was it founded on a unique reappraisal of the contemporary Irish land system. Yet what Ramón has described as "the full extent of [Lalor's] intellectual originality" continues to be overlooked.[7] James Fintan Lalor's contribution to Ireland's intellectual history was significant and should earn him a prominent place in the pantheon of great Irish thinkers.

---

[6] Davitt, *Fall of Feudalism*, p. 58

[7] Marta Ramón, "Writs of ejectment: James Fintan Lalor and the rewriting of nation as physical space, 1847-1848", *Revista Canaria de estudios Ingleses*, 69/ (2014), p. 73.

BIBLIOGRAPHY

Manuscripts and Archives

National Archives of Ireland

1848/105/6   Official papers

National Library of Ireland

Ms. 340   Drafts of speeches by James Fintan Lalor on the land question, Repeal, education, etc., and letters from Lalor to Sir Charles Gavan Duffy, Thomas D'Arcy McGee, John Mitchel, and others, 1844-48

Ms. 8563   A number of letters by James Fintan Lalor to members of the family

Ms. 8570   Rent receipts, household expenses, and other particulars relating to the estates of the Lalor family of Tinakill, Leix, including a lease of lands to the family, 1767 and contemporary notes relating to the birth of James Fintan and other children of Patrick Lalor, 1767 - 1893

Ms. 8562   Correspondence of Patrick Lalor, of Tinakill, Leix, father of James Fintan, with members of his family, and with others, dealing mainly with political subjects, 1825-1854

Ms. 8573   Resolutions for the solution of the land problem proposed by Richard Lalor, together with political, parliamentary and personal items, 1823-1870

Ms. 18,390   Photocopy of letter of James Fintan Lalor to Sir Robert Peel re Repeal agitation; June-July, 1843

Mss. 5756-5757 Letters to Charles Gavan Duffy from people prominent in literary and political affairs, 1840 - 1854

Ms. 20,851   Twentieth-century copies of letters from James Fintan Lalor, mainly to Thomas Clarke Luby, 6 items, 1849, also copy of poem by Fr. Kenyon on Lalor, n.d.

Royal Irish Academy

12.P.15   Gavan Duffy Bequest, box 1

British Parliament

[Hansard], *Parliamentary Debates*, vol. 72, col. 722 (13 Feb. 1844)
[Hansard], *Parliamentary Debates*, vol. 73, col. 237-8 (23 Feb. 1844)
Parliamentary Papers (1831-32), 508, XXI.245, Second report from the select committee of the House of Commons on tithes in Ireland
Parliamentary Papers (1845), XXVIII. [1], Report from Her Majesty's Commissioners of inquiry into the state of the Law and Practice in respect to the Occupation of Land in Ireland
Parliamentary Papers (1845), Cm 657, XXI.1, Evidence taken before Her Majesty's Commissioners of inquiry into the state of the law and practice in respect of the occupation of land in Ireland. Part III

Printed Primary Sources

Collections of the writings of James Fintan Lalor

Fogarty, Lillian, *James Fintan Lalor: Patriot and Political Essayist (1807-1849)*, with a preface by Arthur Griffith (Dublin, 1918),
__, *James Fintan Lalor: Patriot and Political Essayist - Collected Writings*, with a biographical note by L. Fogarty, M. A. (Bean T. Uí Thuama) (Dublin, 1947)
__, *James Fintan Lalor: Patriot and Political Essayist (1807-1849)*, with a preface by Arthur Griffith, ed. John Kelly (Dublin, 1997)
Guarino, Eva, and Turnbull, Judith (eds.), *Collected Writings by and about James Fintan Lalor* (Rome, 1999)
Lalor, James Fintan, "*The Faith of a Felon*" *and other writings*, ed. Marta Ramón (Dublin, 2012)
Marlowe, Nathaniel, *Collected Writings of James Fintan Lalor* (Dublin, 1918)
O'Donoghue, T. G. (ed.), *The Writings of James Fintan Lalor, with an introduction embodying personal recollections by John O'Leary, and a brief memoir* (Dublin, 1895)

Books and articles

The Encyclopaedia Britannica, or, Dictionary of arts, sciences, and general literature, 7th ed., (21 vols, Edinburgh, 1842)
The Spirit of the Nation. By the writers of the Nation newspaper, 2nd ed., (Dublin, 1844)
Beaumont, Gustave de, *Ireland: Social, Political, and Religious*, ed. and tr. William Cooke Taylor (London, 1839)
Bicheno, James Ebenezer, *Ireland and its Economy: Being the Result of Observations Made in a Tour Through the Country in 1829* (London, 1830)

Bibliography

Blackstone, William, *Commentaries on the Laws of England*, 15th edn, ed. Edward Christian, (4 vols, London, 1809)

Cole, G.D.H. and Filson, A.W. (eds.), *British Working Class Movements: Select Documents, 1789-1875* (London, 1951)

Crawford, William Sharman, "Sharman Crawford on Ulster Tenant Right, 1846", ed. Brian A. Kennedy, *Irish Historical Studies*, 13/51, Mar. 1963, pp. 246-53

Davidson, J. Morrison, *Concerning Four Precursors of Henry George and the Single Tax: as also the land gospel according to Winstanley "the Digger"* (London, 1899)

Davis, Thomas, "India - her own and another's", *Dublin Monthly Magazine, being a new series of The Citizen*, 1/4 (Feb. 1840), pp. 255-63

___, "Udalism and Feudalism, I & II", *Dublin Monthly Magazine, being a new series of The Citizen*, Mar/Apr. 1842, pp. 218-37, 293-315

Davitt, Michael, *The Fall of Feudalism in Ireland or the Story of the Land League Revolution* (London, 1904)

Devyr, Thomas Ainge, *The Odd Book of the Nineteenth Century, or, "Chivalry" in modern days, a personal record of reform - chiefly land reform, for the last fifty years.* (New York, 1882)

Doheny, Michael, *The Felon's Track* (New York, 1849)

Duffy, Charles Gavan, *Young Ireland: a Fragment of Irish history, 1840-1850* (London, 1880)

___, *Four Years of Irish History, 1845-1849: a Sequel to "Young Ireland"* (London, 1883)

___, *The League of North and South. An Episode in Irish history, 1850-1854*, (London, 1886)

___, *My Life in Two Hemispheres* (2 vols, New York, 1898)

Edmonds, Cyrus R., *The Life and Times of General Washington* (2 vols, London, 1835-6)

George, Henry, *Progress and Poverty; an inquiry into the cause of industrial depressions, and of increase of want with increase of wealth. The remedy* (New York, 1881)

Kramnick, Isaac (ed.), *The Portable Enlightenment Reader* (London, 1995)

Lewis, George Cornewall, *Remarks on the Third Report of the Irish Poor Inquiry Commissioners* (London, 1837), Dippam

Locke, John, *Two Treatises of Government: in the former the false principles & foundation of Sir Robert Filmer & his followers, are detected & overthrown; the latter is an essay concerning the true original, extent & end of civil government*, 5th ed., (London, 1728)

Marx, Karl and Engels, Friedrich, *The Communist Manifesto* (London, 1985)

Mitchel, John, *Jail Journal, or, Five years in British prisons* (New York, 1854)

___, *The Last Conquest of Ireland (perhaps)* (Glasgow, 1882)

O'Connor, Arthur, *The State of Ireland. To which are added his addresses to the electors of the county of Antrim* (London, 1798)

O'Connor, Feargus, *A Practical Work on the Management of Small Farms*, 4th edn (Manchester, 1846)

Ogilvie, William, *An Essay on the Right of Property in Land: with respect to its foundation in the law of nature, its present establishment by the municipal* laws of Europe, and the regulations by which it might be rendered more beneficial to the lower ranks of mankind (London, 1781)

O'Leary, John, *Recollections of Fenians and Fenianism*, (2 vols., London, 1896)

Paine, Thomas, *Rights of Man. Part the second. Combining principle and practice by Thomas Paine, secretary for foreign affairs to Congress in the American war, and author of the work entitled Common sense; and the first part of the Rights of man.* (Carlisle, 1792)

Pearse, Padraic, *Collected Works of Padraic H. Pearse: Political Writings and Speeches* (Dublin, 1922)

Raumer, Frederick von, *England in 1835: Being a series of letters written to friends in Germany*, tr. Sarah Austin and H. E. Lloyd (3 vols, London, 1836)

Savage, John, *'98 and '48: the Modern Revolutionary History and Literature of Ireland*, 3rd ed. (New York, 1856)

Sillard, P. A., *The Life and Letters of John Martin, with sketches of Thomas Devin Reilly, Fathers John Kenyon, and other "Young Irelanders"*, (Dublin, 1893)

Somerville, Alexander, *The Whistler at the Plough*, (Manchester, 1852)

Thiers, M.A., *The History of the French Revolution*, tr. Frederick Shoberl (5 vols, London, 1838)

University College Dublin, *Calendar for the session 1918-1919* (Dublin, 1919)

Young, Arthur, *A Tour in Ireland* (2 vols, Dublin, 1780)

Pamphlets

Conner, William, *The Speech of William Conner against Rack-Rents, &c., delivered at a meeting at Inch* (Dublin, 1832)

___, *The True Political Economy of Ireland: or rack-rent the one great cause of all her evils: with its remedy. Being a speech delivered at a meeting of the farming classes, at Inch, in the Queen's County* (Dublin, 1835)

___, *The Axe Laid to the Root of Irish Oppression: and a sure and speedy remedy, for the evils of Ireland* (Dublin, 1840)

___, *A Letter to the Tenantry of Ireland: containing an exposition of the rackrent system: and pointing out a valuation and perpetuity as its only effectual remedy* (Dublin, 1850)

Devyr, Thomas Ainge, *Our Natural Rights: a pamphlet for the people* (Belfast, 1836)

Duffy, Charles Gavan, *Letter to John Mitchel* (Dublin, 1854)

Hancock, William Neilson, *The Tenant-Right of Ulster, considered economically: being an essay read before the Dublin University Philosophical Society* (Dublin, 1845)

Mitchel, John, *Memoir of Thomas Devin Reilly: a lecture delivered by John Mitchel, in the Tabernacle, New-York, on Dec. 29th, 1856* (New York, 1857)

___, *Lectures on the Land Tenures of Europe: delivered in the "Swift" Confederate Club, Dublin, on the 18th and 25th of October,1847* (Dublin, 1848)

Paine, Thomas, *Agrarian Justice, opposed to agrarian law, and to agrarian monopoly* (London, 1797)

Russell, Thomas, *A Letter to the People of Ireland, on the present situation of the country* (Belfast, 1796)

Somerville, Alexander, *A Cry from Ireland, or, Landlord and tenant exemplified: a narrative of the proceedings of Richard Shee, Esq. ... against his tenantry at Bennet's Bridge* (London, 1843)

Spence, Thomas, *The Rights of Man, as exhibited in a lecture, read at the Philosophical Society, in Newcastle, to which is now first added an interesting conversation between a gentleman and the author on the subject of his scheme*, 4th ed. (London, 1793)

___, *The End of Oppression; being a dialogue between an old mechanic and a young one. Concerning the establishment of the rights of man* (London, 1795)

___, *The Rights of Infants; or, The imprescriptable right of mothers to such a share of the elements as is sufficient to enable them to suckle and bring up their young. In a dialogue between the aristocracy and a mother of children* (London, 1797)

Workingmen's Association, *The People's Charter; being the outline of an act to provide for the just representation of the people of Great Britain in the Commons House of Parliament* (London, 1838)

Newspapers and Periodicals

Citizen
Cork Examiner
Dublin Evening Post
Dundalk Democrat
Evening Mail
Freeman's Journal
Irish Felon
Irish Nation
Irish Press
Irish Times
Irish Tribune
Irishman
Leinster Express
Lloyd's Evening Post
Nation
National Reformer and Manx Weekly Review of Home and Foreign Affairs
Nenagh Guardian
New York Tribune
Poor Man's Guardian and Repealer's Friend
Times
Tipperary Vindicator
Tribune
Tuam Herald
United Irishman

Printed Secondary Sources

Books and articles

Aalen, F. H. A., "Enclosures in eastern Ireland. A general introduction", *Irish Geography*, 5/2 (1965), pp. 30-35

Allan, David, "'The wisest and most beneficial schemes': William Ogilvie, radical political economy and the Scottish Enlightenment", in Gordon Pentland & Michael T Davis (eds.), *Liberty, Property and Popular Politics: England and Scotland, 1688-1815 : Essays in Honour of H.T. Dickinson* (Edinburgh, 2016), pp. 103-17

Andrews, Ann, *Newspapers and Newsmakers: the Dublin Nationalist Press in the Mid-Nineteenth Century* (Liverpool, 2014)

Barry, E. Eldon, *Nationalisation in British politics: the Historical Background* (London, 1965)

Beer, Max, *The Pioneers of Land Reform: Thomas Spence, William Ogilvie, Thomas Paine, with an introduction by M. Beer* (London, 1920)

Belchem, John, "The neglected "unstamped": the Manx pauper press of the 1840s", *Albion: A Quarterly Journal Concerned with British Studies*, 24/4 (1992), pp. 605-16

Benson, Charles and Fitzpatrick, Siobhán, "Pamphlets", in James H. Murphy (ed.), *The Oxford History of the Irish Book: volume 4: the Irish book in English, 1800-1891* (Oxford, 2011)

Bew, Paul, "The Land League ideal: achievements and contradictions", in P. J. Drudy (ed.), *Ireland: Land, Politics and People* (Cambridge, 1982), pp. 77-92

__, *Conflict and Conciliation in Ireland, 1890-1910: Parnellites and Radical Agrarians* (Oxford, 1987)

Black, R. D. Collison, *Economic Thought and the Irish Question, 1817-1870* (Cambridge, 1960)

Blackshields, Daniel and Considine, John, "Economic thought in Arthur O'Connor's 'The State of Ireland': reducing politics to science", in Tom Boylan, Renee Prendergast and John D. Turner (eds.), *A History of Irish Economic Thought* (London, 2011), pp. 82-106

Bloch, Marc, *The Historian's Craft*, (Manchester, 1992)

Bloy, Marjorie, "Lalor, James Fintan", in Brian Lalor (ed.), *The Encyclopaedia of Ireland* (Dublin, 2003), p. 604

Blum, Jerome, "English parliamentary enclosure", *Journal of Modern History*, 53/3 (1981), pp. 477-504

Boyce, D. George, *Nineteenth Century Ireland: the Search for Stability*, 2nd edn (Dublin, 2005)

Boylan, Thomas and Foley, Timothy, "From hedge school to hegemony: intellectuals, ideology and Ireland in nineteenth-century Ireland", in Liam O'Dowd (ed.), *On Intellectuals and Intellectual Life in Ireland: International, Comparative and Historical Contexts* (Belfast, 1996), pp. 98-115

Bronstein, Jamie L., *Land Reform and Working-class Experience in Britain and the United States, 1800-1862* (Stanford, Calif., 1999)

Buckley, David N., *James Fintan Lalor: Radical* (Cork, 1990)
Bull, Philip, *Land, Politics and Nationalism: a Study of the Irish Land Question* (Dublin, 1996)
Chapman, John, "The extent and nature of parliamentary enclosure", *Agricultural History Review*, 35/1 (1987), pp. 25-35
Chase, Malcolm, *The People's Farm: English Radical Agrarianism, 1775-1840* (Oxford, 1988)
___, "Chartism and the land: 'The mighty People's Question'", in Matthew Cragoe and Paul Readman (eds.), *The Land Question in Britain, 1750-1950* (Basingstoke, 2010), pp. 57-73
Christianson, Gale E., "Secret societies and agrarian violence in Ireland, 1790-1840", *Agricultural History*, 46/3 (1972), pp. 369-84
Clark, J. C. D., *Thomas Paine: Britain, America, and France in the Age of Enlightenment and Revolution* (Oxford, 2018)
Comerford, R.V., "The Land War and the politics of distress, 1877–82" in W. E. Vaughan (ed.), *A New History of Ireland, Volume VI: Ireland Under the Union, II: 1870-1921* (Oxford, 2010), pp. 26-52
Crotty, Raymond, *Irish Agricultural Production: its Volume and Structure* (Cork, 1966)
Daly, Mary E., "James Fintan Lalor (1807-1849) and rural revolution", in Ciaran, Brady (ed.), *Worsted in the Game: Losers in Irish history* (Dublin, 1989), pp. 111-19
Dickinson, H. T., *Bolingbroke* (London, 1970)
Dickson, David, "Paine and Ireland", in David Dickson, Daire Keogh and Kevin Whelan (eds.), *The United Irishmen: Republicanism, Radicalism and Rebellion* (Dublin, 1993), pp. 135-50
Dillon, William, *Life of John Mitchel* (2 vols, London, 1888)
Donnelly, James S., "The Whiteboy movement, 1761-5", *Irish Historical Studies*, 21/81 (1978), pp. 20-54
Dooley, Terence, "Land and the people", in Alvin Jackson (ed.), *Oxford Handbook of Modern Irish History* (Oxford, 2014), pp. 107-25, Oxford Handbooks Online
Duddy, Thomas, *A History of Irish Thought* (London, 2002)
Eayrs, James, "The political ideas of the English agrarians, 1775-1815", *Canadian Journal of Economics and Political Science*, 18/3 (1952), pp. 287-302
Ferriter, Diarmaid, *The Transformation of Ireland 1900-2000* (London, 2005)
Foster, R. F., *Modern Ireland 1600-1972* (London, 1989)
Fruchtman Jr., Jack, "Foreword", in Sidney Hook (ed.), *Common Sense, Rights of Man, and Other Essential Writings of Thomas Paine* (New York, 2003)
Garvin, Tom and Hess, Andreas, "Gustave de Beaumont: Ireland's Alexis de Tocqueville", in Séamas Ó Síocháin (ed.), *Social Thought on Ireland in the Nineteenth Century* (Dublin, 2009), pp. 9-26
Goldring, Maurice, *Pleasant the Scholar's Life: Irish Intellectuals and the Construction of the Nation State* (London, 1993)
Gray, Peter, "Lalor, James Fintan" in Sean J. Connolly (ed.), *The Oxford Companion to Irish History* (Oxford, 1998), p. 294

___, *Famine, Land, and Politics: British Government and Irish Society, 1843-1850* (Dublin, 1999)

___, "The peculiarities of Irish land tenure, 1800-1914: from agent of impoverishment to agent of pacification", in Donald Norman Winch and Patrick Karl O'Brien (eds.), *The Political Economy of British Historical Experience, 1688-1914* (Oxford, 2002), pp. 139-64

Hanson, Paul R., *Historical Dictionary of the French Revolution*, 2nd edn (Lanham, 2015)

Harding, Neil, "Marx, Engels and the Manifesto: working class, party, and proletariat, *Journal of Political Ideologies*, 3/1 (1998), pp. 13-44.

Hickey, D. J. and Doherty, J. E. (eds.), *A Dictionary of Irish History* (Dublin, 1987)

Holcombe, Randall G., *From Liberty to Democracy: the Transformation of American Government* (Ann Arbor, MI., 2002)

Hoppen, K. Theodore, *Ireland since 1800: Conflict and Conformity* (Harlow, 1999)

Horne, Thomas A., *Property Rights and Poverty: Political Argument in Britain, 1605-1834* (London, 1990)

Jones, Colin, *The Longman Companion to the French Revolution* (Harlow, 1988)

Kelly, James, "Reviewed Work(s): James Fintan Lalor: Radical by David N. Buckley", *Studia Hibernica*, /26 (1992), pp. 255-7

Kinealy, Christine, *Repeal and Revolution: 1848 in Ireland* (Oxford, 2009)

King, Carla, "Review: James Fintan Lalor by Thomas P. O'Neill", *Books Ireland*, /270 (2004), pp. 231-2

Knowlton, Steven R., "The quarrel between Gavan Duffy and John Mitchel: implications for Ireland", *Albion: A Quarterly Journal Concerned with British Studies*, 21/4 (1989), pp. 581-90

Knox, Thomas R., "Thomas Spence: The Trumpet of Jubilee", *Past & Present*, /76 (1977), pp. 75-98

Lee, J. J., *The Modernisation of Irish Society 1848-1918* (Dublin, 2008)

Leerssen, Joep, *Remembrance and Imagination: Patterns in the Historical and Literary Representation of Ireland in the Nineteenth Century* (Cork, 1996)

Lyons, F. S. L., *Ireland since the Famine* (London, 1973)

MacAskill, Joy, "The Chartist Land Plan", in Asa Briggs (ed.), *Chartist Studies* (London, 1959), pp. 304-41

Mathias, Peter, *The First Industrial Nation: an Economic History of Britain 1700-1914* (London, 1983)

McCaffrey, Lawrence J., *Daniel O'Connell and the Repeal Year* (Kentucky, 1966)

McGovern, Bryan P., *John Mitchel: Irish Nationalist, Southern Secessionist* (Knoxville, 2009)

McMahon, Timothy, "'The land for the people': the Irish Revolution as a revolution of rising expectations", in Michael De Nie and Sean Farrell (eds.), *Power and Popular Culture in Modern Ireland: Essays in Honour of James S. Donnelly, Jr.* (Dublin, 2010), pp. 172-92

Mingay, Gordon E., *Parliamentary Enclosure in England: an Introduction to its Causes, Incidence and Impact 1750-1850* (London, 1997)

Monaghan, Patricia, *The Encyclopedia of Celtic Mythology and Folklore* (New York, 2004)

Moore, Tony, "Citizens of the world: Paine and the political prisoners transported to Australia", in Sam Edwards and Marcus Morris (eds.), *The Legacy of Thomas Paine in the Transatlantic World* (Abingdon, 2017), pp. 151-70

Moynihan, Maurice (ed.), *Speeches and Statements by Eamon de Valera, 1917-73* (Dublin, 1980)

Nevin, Donal, *James Larkin: Lion of the Fold* (Dublin, 1998)

Murphy, James H., *Abject Loyalty: Nationalism and Monarchy in Ireland during the Reign of Queen Victoria* (Cork, 2001)

O'Brien, George, "William Conner", *Studies*, 12/46 (1923), pp. 279-89

O'Brien, Richard Barry, *Thomas Drummond: Under-Secretary in Ireland, 1835-40; Life and Letters* (London, 1889)

O'Day, Alan, *Irish Home Rule, 1867-1921* (Manchester, 1998)

O'Donoghue, Patrick, "Causes of the opposition to tithes, 1830-38", *Studia Hibernica*, /5 (1965), pp. 7-28

O'Higgins, Rachel, "The Irish influence in the Chartist Movement", *Past & Present*, /20 (1961), pp. 83-96

O'Neill, Thomas Patrick, "The papers of James Fintan Lalor in the National Library", *Irish Book Lover*, 30/4 (1948), pp. 84-86

__, "The economic and political ideas of James Fintan Lalor", *Irish Ecclesiastical Record*, 74/ (1950), pp. 398-409

__, "The Irish Land Question, 1830-1850", *Studies*, 44/175 (1955), pp. 325-36

__, *James Fintan Lalor*, tr. John T. Goulding (Wexford, 2003). First published as Tomás P. Ó Néill, *Fiontán Ó Leathlobhair* (Dublin, 1962)

O'Shannon, Cathal, "James Fintan Lalor", in M. J., MacManus (ed.), *Thomas Davis and Young Ireland* (Dublin, 1945), pp. 68-70

Parssinen, T. M., "Thomas Spence and the origins of English land nationalization", *Journal of the History of Ideas*, 34/1 (1973), pp. 135-41

Plack, Noelle, "The peasantry, feudalism, and the environment, 1789-93", in Peter McPhee (ed.), *A Companion to the French Revolution* (Somerset, 2012), pp. 212-228

Plummer, Alfred, *Bronterre: a Political Biography of Bronterre O'Brien, 1804-1864* (London, 1971)

Pomfret, John E., *The Struggle for Land in Ireland, 1800-1923* (Princeton, 1930), HeinOnline Legal Classics

Quinn, James, *Young Ireland and the Writing of Irish History* (Dublin, 2015)

Ramón, Marta, "Writs of ejectment: James Fintan Lalor and the rewriting of nation as physical space, 1847-1848", *Revista Canaria de estudios Ingleses*, /69 (2014), pp. 71-82

Riall, Lucy, *Garibaldi: Invention of a Hero* (New Haven, 2007)

Rudkin, Olive Durant, *Thomas Spence and his Connections* (London, 1927)

Sabine, B.E.V., *History of Income Tax: the Development of Income Tax from its Beginning in 1799 to the Present Day related to the Social, Economic and Political History of the Period* (Oxford, 2006)

Shields, Andrew, "From repeal to revolution: the evolution of John Mitchel's political thought 1843–48", in Anders Ahlqvist and Pamela O'Neill (eds.), *Language and Power in the Celtic World: papers from the seventh Australian*

Conference of Celtic Studies, University of Sydney, September 2010 (Sydney, 2010), pp. 409-424

Skinner, Quentin, "Meaning and understanding in the history of ideas", *History and Theory*, 8/1 (1969), pp. 3-53

Smyth, Jim, *The Men of No Property: Irish Radicals and Popular Politics in the Late Eighteenth Century* (Basingstoke, 1998)

Sokol, Mary, "Jeremy Bentham and the real property commission of 1828", *Utilitas*, 4/2 (1992), pp. 225-45

Sperber, Jonathan, "The Atlantic revolutions in the German lands, 1776–1849", in Helmut Walser Smith (ed.), *The Oxford Handbook of Modern German History* (Oxford, 2011)

Stephenson, Carl, *Mediaeval Feudalism* (Ithaca, 1956)

Thompson, E. P., *The Making of the English Working Class* (New York, 1963)

Thompson, S. J., "Parliamentary enclosure, property, population, and the decline of classical republicanism in eighteenth-century Britain", *The Historical Journal*, 51/3 (2008), pp. 621-42

Turner, Michael J., "Ireland and Irishness in the political thought of Bronterre O'Brien", *Irish Historical Studies*, 39/153 (2014), pp. 40-57

___, *Radicalism and Reputation: the Career of Bronterre O'Brien* (East Lansing, MI, 2017)

Uí Chollatáin, R., "P. H. Pearse deeply influenced by writings of James Fintan Lalor", *Laois Heritage Society Journal*, 3/ (2006), pp. 24-35

Ünal, Fatma Gül, *Land Ownership Inequality and Rural Factor Markets in Turkey: a Study for Critically Evaluating Market Friendly Reforms* (New York, 2012)

Williams, Nicholas, "Literature in Irish", in S. J. Connolly (ed.), *The Oxford Companion to Irish History*, 2nd edn (Oxford, 2002)

Wilson, David, *Thomas D'Arcy McGee: Passion, Reason, and Politics, 1825-1857, vol. 1* (Montreal, 2008)

Unpublished theses

O'Brien, Michael G., "The Lalors of Tenakill 1767-1893" (M.A. thesis, St. Patrick's College, Maynooth, 1987)

Tally, Patrick Francis, "The growth of the Dublin weekly press and the development of Irish nationalism, 1810–1879" (PhD thesis, University of Wisconsin-Madison, 2003)

Electronic Resources

Cronin, Maura, "O'Connor, Fergus (Feargus)", *Dictionary of Irish Biography* (Cambridge, 2009), (http://dib.cambridge.org/viewReadPage.do?articleId=a6589) 17 Feb. 2018

D'Arcy, Fergus A., "O'Brien, James ('Bronterre')", *Dictionary of Irish Biography* (Cambridge, 2009), (http://dib.cambridge.org/viewReadPage.do?articleId=a6474) 17 Feb. 2018

Bibliography

Daly, Mary E., "Lalor, James Fintan", *Dictionary of Irish Biography*, (Cambridge, 2009), (http://dib.cambridge.org/viewReadPage.do?articleId=a4646) 30 Mar. 2017

Dickinson, H. T. "Spence, Thomas (1750–1814), radical and bookseller", *Oxford Dictionary of National Biography*, (http://ezproxy-prd.bodleian.ox.ac.uk:2167/view/10.1093/ref:odnb/9780198614128.001.0001/odnb-9780198614128-e-26112) 15 Jan. 2018

Fellmeth, Aaron X. and Horwitz, Maurice, "Nullum tempus occurrit regi" *Guide to Latin in International Law* (Oxford, 2009), [http://www.oxfordreference.com/view/10.1093/acref/9780195369380.001.0001/acref-9780195369380-e-1499] 21 Jul. 2017

Frykenberg, Robert Eric, "Malcolm, Sir John (1769–1833), diplomatist and administrator in India." *Oxford Dictionary of National Biography*, [http://ezproxy-prd.bodleian.ox.ac.uk:2167/view/10.1093/ref:odnb/9780198614128.001.0001/odnb-9780198614128-e-17864] 6 Mar. 2019

Geoghegan, Patrick M. and Quinn, James, "O'Doherty, Kevin Izod", *Dictionary of Irish Biography* (Cambridge, 2009), (http://dib.cambridge.org/viewReadPage.do?articleId=a6680), 24 Feb. 2018

Hourican, Bridget, "Lalor, Patrick ('Patt')", *Dictionary of Irish Biography* (Cambridge, 2009), (http://dib.cambridge.org/viewReadPage.do?articleId=a4646) 30 Mar. 2017

Maume, Patrick, "Conner, William", *Dictionary of Irish Biography* (Cambridge, 2009), (http://dib.cambridge.org/viewReadPage.do?articleId=a1950) 4 May 2018

__, "Duffy, Sir Charles Gavan", *Dictionary of Irish Biography* (Cambridge, 2009), (http://dib.cambridge.org/viewReadPage.do?articleId=a2808) 11 Jun. 2018

__, "O'Neill, Thomas Patrick", *Dictionary of Irish Biography* (Cambridge, 2009), (http://dib.cambridge.org/viewReadPage.do?articleId=a6941) 15 Feb. 2017

Philp, Mark. "Paine, Thomas (1737–1809), author and revolutionary", *Oxford Dictionary of National Biography*, (http://ezproxy-prd.bodleian.ox.ac.uk:2167/view/10.1093/ref:odnb/9780198614128.001.0001/odnb-9780198614128-e-21133) 21 Jan. 2018

Prest, Wilfrid, "Blackstone, Sir William (1723–1780)", *Oxford Dictionary of National Biography*, [http://ezproxy-prd.bodleian.ox.ac.uk:2167/view/article/2536] 20 July 2017

Quinn, James, "Crawford, William Sharman", *Dictionary of Irish Biography* (Cambridge, 2009), (http://dib.cambridge.org/viewReadPage.do?articleId=a2168) 19 Feb. 2018

__, "Mitchel, John", *Dictionary of Irish Biography* (Cambridge, 2012), (http://dib.cambridge.org/viewReadPage.do?articleId=a5834) 6 Jun. 2017

__, "Reilly, Thomas Devin", *Dictionary of Irish Biography* (Cambridge, 2009), (http://dib.cambridge.org/viewReadPage.do?articleId=a7626) 17 Jul. 2017

Ritchie, Lionel Alexander. "Ogilvie, William (1736–1819), classical scholar and advocate of common property in land." *Oxford Dictionary of National Biography*, (http://ezproxy-prd.bodleian.ox.ac.uk:2167/view/10.1093/ref:odnb/9780198614128.001.0001/odnb-9780198614128-e-20589) 3 Mar. 2018

FURTHER READING

Armitage, David, "A patriot for whom? The afterlives of Bolingbroke's Patriot King", *Journal of British Studies*, 36/4 (1997), pp. 397-418

Blacker, William, *The Claims of the Landed Interests to Legislative Protection Considered*, (London, 1836)

Bolingbroke, Henry St. John, *Letters, on the Spirit of Patriotism, on the Idea of a Patriot King, and on the State of Parties, at the Accession of King George the First* (London, 1749)

Carlyle, Thomas, *Past and Present* (London, 1843)

Connolly, James, *Labour in Irish History* (Dublin, 1914)

Dickinson, H. T., *Liberty and Property: Political Ideology in 18th Century Britain* (London, 1977)

Kramnick, Isaac, *Bolingbroke and his Circle: the Politics of Nostalgia in the Age of Walpole* (Cambridge, Mass., 1968)

Madden, R. R., *The United Irishmen, Their Lives and Times*, 3rd series (3 vols, Dublin, 1846)

Marx, Karl and Engels, Friedrich, *Ireland and the Irish Question* (Moscow, 1971)

Mowat, C. L., "Review: Nationalisation in British Politics: the Historical Background by R. Eldon Barry", *The American Historical Review*, 71/2 (1966), pp. 567-8

O'B., G., "Reviewed Work(s): James Fintan Lalor, Patriot and Political Essayist by L. Fogarty; James Fintan Lalor, Collected Writings by Nathaniel M. Marlowe", *Studies*, 8/31 (1919), pp. 494-5

Thompson, William, *An Inquiry into the Principles of the Distribution of Wealth Most Conducive to Human Happiness; applied to the newly proposed system of voluntary equality of wealth* (London, 1824)

INDEX

1798 Rebellion, xii, 45, 59, 61

A

allodium, 1, 24
American War of Independence, 56
Attila the Hun, 78

B

Ballingarry. *See* Young Ireland
Barbeyrac, Jean, 79
Beaumont, Gustave de, 2–3
Bentham, Jeremy, 48
Blacker, William, 45
Blackstone, William, 1, 2, 41, 76–79, 92
Bolingbroke, Henry St John, 1st Viscount, 47–48
Brenan, Joseph, 48, 122, 127
British legislation
    Act of Union (1800), 14, 15, 22, 45, 108
    Convention Act (1793), 22
    Crown of Ireland Act (1542), 41
    Land Law (Ireland) Act (1881), 100
    Landlord and Tenant (Ireland) Act (1870), 100
British Museum, 12
Buonarroti, Philippe
    History of Babeuf's Conspiracy for Equality, 68
Butt, Isaac, 97

C

Carlow College, 47
Carlyle, Thomas, 44
Chartism, 46, 62, 63, 64, 65, 67, 69, 121
Clarendon, Earl of (Lord Lieutenant of Ireland), 106
Coke, Edward, 1
Commentaries on the Laws of England. *See* Blackstone, William
Conner, William, 40, 85–89, 99, 101, 122
Connolly, James, 6, 7
Crawford, William Sharman, 63, 86, 89–90, 94, 99, 101
Cromwellian conquest, 4, 51
Crotty, Raymond, ix, 42

D

Davis, Thomas, 17, 21, 45, 69–72, 76, 80, 116, 128
Davitt, Michael, ix, x, 9, 11, 42, 97, 125–26, 128
de Valera, Éamon, 42
Devon Commission, 3–5, 48–49, 92, 93, 96
Devyr, Thomas Ainge, 62–63, 65
Digby, Kenelm Thomas, 96
Diggers, The, 49
Dillon, John Blake, 17
Doheny, Michael, x, 26–27, 27, 28, 29, 41, 85, 98, 101–4, 105, 106, 111, 118, 119, 123

Domesday Book, 78
Drummond, Thomas, 2–3, 92
Duffy, Charles Gavan, 33, 36, 80
    relationship with JFL, xi, 5, 15–17, 17, 18, 20, 22–23, 29, 34, 35, 36, 43, 45, 101, 104, 107, 108, 109, 112, 115, 118, 123
    relationship with John Mitchel, 21, 24, 108, 109, 112, 114–15, 117, 118
    Tenant League, 98–101, 126
    The Nation, 17, 33, 76, 98, 120

E

Easter Rising (1916), 11, 127
Emmet, Robert, xii, 45
Encyclopaedia Britannica, 1, 77
Engels, Friedrich, 68
Ériu, 39

F

Famine (1845-49), ix, 5, 12, 14, 16–19, 20–22, 25, 35, 42, 43, 57, 66, 68, 73, 80–81, 83, 93, 98, 101, 105, 107, 109, 116, 128
Ferguson, Adam, 52
Fitzgerald, Lord Edward, 45
Frederick William III (Prussia), 116
French Revolution, 20, 35, 39, 56, 57, 60, 61, 68, 72, 73, 92, 127, 128
French Revolution (1830), 8, 73
French Revolution (1848), 8, 73, 74

G

George, Henry, ix, 10, 42, 53, 55, 57, 97
Gladstone, William Ewart, 96, 100, 103

Grattan's Parliament, 45, 113
Griffith, Arthur, 23
Grotius, Hugo, 46, 79

H

Hardenberg, Karl August von, 116
Harney, George Julian, 68
Hely, Charles, 94
Hobbes, Thomas, 46
Holy Cross
    aftermath, 28, 93, 95, 97, 101–2, 112, 119
    meeting, 27–28, 55, 63, 83, 85, 87–88, 88, 89, 92, 99, 101, 102, 111, 123
    prelude, 25–26, 26, 89, 94, 101, 110, 115
Hope, James, 45

I

Irish Confederation, x, 15–18, 20–24, 26–27, 29, 32, 33, 38, 40, 41, 55, 80, 84, 85, 87, 97, 98, 101–2, 104–5, 108, 109, 111–12, *See also* Young Ireland
Irish Free State, ix
Irish National Land League. *See* Land League
Irish Polytechnic Institute, 74

K

King's College, Aberdeen, 50

L

Lalor, Anna (née Dillon), 90
Lalor, James Fintan
    biographical details, x–xi, 6, 9, 14, 36, 44, 46–48, 50, 64, 65,

Index 145

68, 73, 79, 80, 83, 87, 90–91, 95, 96, 105, 119, 120, 127, 128
queen-metaphor, 38–41, 80, 103, 113
Lalor, Jerome, 90
Lalor, Joseph, 90
Lalor, Patrick ('Patt'), 5, 13–14, 17, 65, 67, 90–97, 99, 122
Lalor, Richard, 8, 25, 47, 95–97, 110
Land League, ix, x, 11, 100, 125
Land League of Mayo, 125
Land War, 97
Larkin, James, 42
Lenihan, Maurice, 47, 119, 127
Lewis, George Cornewall, 2
List, Friedrich, 44
Locke, John, 48, 77–79
Loyal National Repeal Association, x, 13, 14–15, 17, 22, 23, 26, 40, 42, 52, 67, 86–87, 88, 94, 95, 100, 109
Luby, Thomas Clarke, 5, 36–37, 47, 48, 73, 91, 110–11, 112, 114, 119, 120

M

MacGrady, James, 28, 86, 93
Mangan, James Clarence, 39, 80
Manifesto of the Communist Party. *See* Marx, Karl
Marnell, John, 15, 17, 43, 83–85, 86, 89
Martin, John, 29–31, 41, 85
Marx, Karl, 7, 68, 75, 76
Mazzini, Giuseppe, 29
McGee, Thomas D'Arcy, 17, 22, 24, 27, 34, 38, 40, 80, 98
Mill, John Stuart, 44
Milner, John, 48
Milton, John, 48

Mitchel, John, 8, 11, 17, 21, 22, 23, 24–25, 27, 31, 34, 38, 78, 80, 104, 109, 128
and the land question, 34, 109, 115–17
arrest and transportation, 29–30, 36, 98, 104, 105, 106, 107, 114, 119
influence of JFL, xi, 11, 21, 25, 101, 106, 108, 109–15, 115–17, 117–18, 118, 119, 122, 123
relationship with Charles Gavan Duffy. *See* Charles Gavan Duffy
The Nation, 107
The United Irishman, 111, 112

N

National Graves Association, x
National Library of Ireland, 8
Newgate Prison, 36, 97, 98, 120

O

O'Brien, James 'Bronterre', 12, 64–69, 71, 72, 74, 80, 84, 93, 121, 128
O'Brien, William Smith, 15, 20, 36, 110, 115
O'Connell, Daniel, 4, 5, 14–15, 15, 17, 22, 23, 26, 40, 65, 67, 68, 86–87, 90, 94, 127
O'Connell, John, 26, 95, 100, 102, 118
O'Connor, Arthur, 60, 63, 86
O'Connor, Feargus, 63–64, 65, 86, 121
O'Hegarty, P. S., 105
O'Leary, John, 36, 118

Ogilvie, William, 12, 50–53, 54, 55, 57, 58, 64, 93
Osborne, Ralph Bernal, 107–8
Owen, Robert, 44

P

Paine, Thomas, 56–58, 93
   and Ireland, 58–59, 59–61, 62, 64
Parnell, Charles Stewart, ix
Pearse, Patrick, 6, 7, 11, 127
Peel, Sir Robert, 3, 12–13, 71
Penal Laws, 4
Phillip III, King (Spain)
   expulsion of the Moriscos, 51
Physiocrats, 44
Prussia (land reforms), 116–17
Pufendorf, Samuel von, 46, 79

Q

Quesnay, François. *See* Physiocrats

R

Reformation (English), 4, 51
Reilly, Thomas Devin, 25, 29, 30, 101, 104–6, 111, 118, 119, 123
Repeal Association. *See* Loyal National Repeal Association
Ribbonmen, The, 91
Russell, Lord John, 3
Russell, Thomas, 60

S

Savage, John, 119
Scott, Walter, x, 47, 48
Scrope, George Poulett, 44
Segrave, Michael, 121
Shee, Richard, 3, 5

Smith, Adam, 52
Somerville, Alexander, 3
Spence, Thomas, 12, 53–59, 61–62, 64, 65, 71, 72, 74, 80, 84, 93
   Spencean Philantropists, 59, 64
Stein, Karl Freiherr von, 116

T

tenant right. *See* Ulster Custom
Thompson, William, 45
Thornton, William Thomas, 44
Times, The (London), 26, 28, 33, 83
Tithe War, 91–92, 96
Tone, Theobald Wolfe, xii, 45
Trinity College Dublin (TCD), 64, 80
Trinity Street (*Irish Felon* office), 33, 75

U

Udalism. *See* Davis, Thomas
Ulster Custom, 11, 14, 27, 28, 30, 32, 33, 34, 37, 44, 63, 71, 86, 88, 89, 97, 99, 100, 110
United Irishmen, 45, 59, 60, 61, 80, 109, 122
University College Dublin (UCD), 8

V

Victoria, Queen, 40–41, 88, 102, 114

W

Whiteboys, The, 2, 50, 91
Williamite war, 4
Wordsworth, William, x, 47, 48

Y

Yeats, William Butler, 41
Young Ireland, 7, 10, 15, 17, 38, 42, 67, 80, 85, 97, 107, 113, 118, 119, 121, 122, *See also* individual entries on Brenan, Doheny, Duffy, Martin, McGee, Mitchel, O'Brien (W.), and Reilly. Ballingarry rebellion, x, 12, 97, 98, 104, 106

www.ingramcontent.com/pod-product-compliance
Lightning Source LLC
Chambersburg PA
CBHW052050300426
44117CB00012B/2060